D1533276

I Will Take You Home

I hope you will
get involved in
helping us save
them all,

Cyrille

I Will Take You Home

REBECCA CUPCAKE TINNES

Charleston, SC
www.PalmettoPublishing.com

I Will Take You Home
Copyright © 2021 by Rebecca Cupcake Tinnes

All rights reserved
No portion of this book may be reproduced, stored in a retrieval system, or transmitted
in any form by any means—electronic, mechanical, photocopy, recording, or other—except
for brief quotations in printed reviews, without prior permission of the author.

First Edition

Paperback ISBN: 978-1-68515-069-3
eBook ISBN: 978-1-68515-070-9

Contents

This book is dedicated to my best friend, Linda Osborne.

I am deeply grateful for our incredibly supportive friendship, our unbelievable, crazed animal adventures, and for all the tear-jerking laughter we have shared. Your friendship is by far the greatest gift in my life.
None of these stories would have been possible without you.

Preface

I was born with an over-exuberant personality, tons of energy, and a wild, almost uncontrollable sense of humor. It's no real surprise that trouble seems to find me. I was also born with a deep love and affection for animals, and that has grounded me throughout my life.

It was more than thirty years ago when the idea of writing a book came to me. My original thought was to create a photo book of people with their cats and dogs to celebrate the universal love we have for animals. That would have been too easy. I nixed that idea and set my heart on writing short, captivating stories to entertain animal-loving readers. With the attention span of a fruit fly and absolutely zero writing skills, I ended up with hundreds of failed attempts.

My frustration led me to attend writing seminars and weekend retreats with published authors. Regrettably, I tortured countless private coaches, editors, and friends during my learning process. And while I was learning the skills to create this book, I was meeting the characters—people, cats, dogs—who ultimately found their way into the pages of what you now hold in your hands.

My inner guide—or whatever you're comfortable calling it, be it God or the universe— made me acutely aware that this book was predestined and was much greater than me. More easily said, it was fated—something I must complete in this life. Why? Because I know the killing of hundreds of thousands of animals each year in shelters is a problem we can solve. Fortunately, since beginning work on this book, the numbers of animals euthanized in shelters has declined from multiple millions each year. One of the solutions is spaying and neutering, and it is my mission to increase access to clinics offering these services as a way to reduce and ultimately eliminate the need for euthanasia in shelters. My hope is that this book will play a role in that effort and enlighten you on the other proven programs that will help turn our country into a no-kill nation.

And so, it is with tremendous pride and overwhelming gratitude to my patient teachers that you hold this book in your hands. Please humor me here: Picture me in a tall, black top hat with a megaphone in my hand as I shout at the top of my lungs, "Ladies and gentlemen, on with the show!"

Introduction

The Beginning

It was 1989. I was in my early twenties and had left behind my childhood home in the Midwest to make my way to Wyoming. Born with
a giving nature, and as a caretaker to elderly and disabled people, I
dreamed of making a positive difference in this world with my life.
Shortly after I arrived in the valley of Jackson Hole, Wyoming, I heard
about a small no-kill shelter in Driggs, Idaho, just over Teton Pass, only
forty minutes away. My strong affection for animals stirred my curiosity: I wanted to help their cats and dogs.

I took home my first foster dog from the Driggs shelter, but it was
not enough for me—or for them—to help just one animal. In my efforts to find loving homes for more animals, I set up mobile adoption
events in Jackson Hole. My adoption events attracted a cast of clever,
talented, and hilarious characters. Our adoptions grew quickly, and
animals found homes like a wildfire throughout the valley. After just
a few of these events, we had placed over two hundred kittens, cats,
puppies, and dogs.

Those successful adoption events fueled my fire to host more events
that showcased the shelter animals. With the goal of raising more
awareness and finding more potential adopters, I held a fashion show,
a dance party, and a wine tasting where we auctioned off a helicopter
trip flown by Harrison Ford (yeah, *that* Harrison Ford).

Not long after those huge gatherings, people began referring to me
as the puppy pusher, the crazy cat lady, or the dog lady. But it was my
extreme sensitivity and quick tendency for tears that gave my longtime,

loveable boyfriend, Olaf, the idea to nickname me Cupcake. He was strong and sensible and repeatedly encouraged me when I got overly emotional by saying, "You better toughen up, ya little Cupcake. It's a harsh, cruel world out there, and sometimes you have to be brave." My close friends call me Cupper but, like my pets, I answer to many names.

Eventually I was given a position on the board of directors at the Driggs Animal Shelter in Idaho. Later, I was offered a position on the board of directors with a group called PAWS in Jackson. I grew disinterested as neither group shared my vision or goals. No matter how many animals we placed in Jackson, the Driggs shelter was always at full capacity. This became a thorn in my side, and it festered. I wanted to know how to increase adoptions. Acting as a freelance volunteer, I independently attended Best Friends Animal Society conventions with the nation's leading experts. It was here that I learned the programs which would later become the foundation for the Animal Adoption Center, the organization I ultimately established in Jackson.

When Things Got Serious . . .

Back in the nineties when Amazon, the internet, and cell phones had not yet taken over our world, many Jacksonites regularly drove over two mountain passes to Idaho Falls, Idaho, to shop at big-box stores like Home Depot or Target, a round-trip drive of over one hundred miles. On the outskirts of town sat a large animal shelter that I had passed on a few of my shopping trips, but I'd always looked away out of fear. This facility killed their cats and dogs when they needed space.

So it took me a few years—and the love of my first foster dog—to gather up the courage to approach the animal shelter in Idaho Falls. As I drove by on what was supposed to be a day of fun shopping, I heard in my mind Olaf's words, "toughen up," and made a split-second decision to take a quick right-hand turn. Pulling up to the plain, white, brick government building surrounded by an intimidating chain link fence, my thought was: Pull a dog, foster it, and adopt it into a great home. It would be a quick in-and-out. I would select a dog now, and then pick it up on my way back home. Afterall, I'd planned for today to be all about me, buying things I'd worked hard for—a pair of pretty pearl earrings, quality makeup from the mall, new jeans, maybe even a new pair of boots!

I heard the faint barking of dogs when I stepped out of the car. My stomach grew tight and anxious. I pulled my shoulders back and told myself to be confident, and followed a set of muddy footprints to the front door.

Standing inside was a heavyset man with a weathered face wearing overalls. His boots were caked in muddy manure, and with him was a matted black-and-white border collie with orange baling twine wrapped around its neck. The farmer shook his fist in the air at the officers behind the counter and yelled, "You're telling me I got to give you fifteen dollars for some surrender fee to dump this good-for-nothing dog off here? That's nothing but highway robbery when a bullet only costs me twenty cents!" He yanked on the twine and clomped back outside to his truck. Instinctively, I quickly followed behind him and said in a strong, loud voice, "Hey, mister! Do you need me to take the dog?"

He said, "Young lady, this dog doesn't work! She's no good."

I replied, "Maybe she's no good to you, but I don't have any cows, so the dog doesn't need to work for me."

"Well, all right then. It will save me a bullet." He shoved his hand in my direction and said, "You can have her."

I walked the collie to my car, leaned against the door, and crouched down beside her, placing my arms loosely around her neck. Her eyes stayed on the farmer as he pulled onto the road and drove away. I wondered what her thoughts were. After he was out of sight, she looked at me, tilted her head, and put her paw on my foot.

The pretty, black-faced border collie with smart brown eyes seemed to smile when I said, "You're all right now. I will take good care of you, baby." She appeared to understand my words, she licked my hand, and wiggled her entire body. I told her to "load up" and she jumped into the back of my SUV. I laughed and said, "Your working days are over, girl. Maybe you would like a tennis ball or a Frisbee? How about a nice bath at Petco to make you feel good? Today is the first day of your new life."

In less than a minute, my innocent stop at the shelter had saved a beautiful dog from a bullet. I could have left with this one dog, but that's not my way of doing things. With a deep sense of gratitude and genuine confidence, I cheerfully and confidently walked back into the building.

When I swung open the front door, the big officer behind the counter asked gruffly, "Are you taking that dog?"

I said, "Yes, I am a volunteer at the animal shelter in Driggs, and I was wondering if you might need a foster parent for any of your other animals?"

The large man wore a gold badge and a name tag: John Parker. He was in his mid-fifties, had a powerful voice, and weighed about 250 pounds. His balding head was shaved down to his scalp. In his uniform, he looked like a cop, and a bit like *Mr. Clean*.

He smiled and said, "Well, go in the back and help yourself. We're pretty full now. The vet will be here later today to clean 'em out and make room for more coming in. Head down the hall. They're all behind the big metal door."

The combination of the putrid stench and the dogs' shrill barking almost knocked me over. I pulled my shirt over my nose and held my breath, then I pushed my fingertips into my ears. I hesitated a moment before I took the steps that changed my life forever. Nothing could have prepared me for what I had found behind that heavy metal door.

The first kennel held a dozen eight-week-old precious puppies squirming with dried poop all over them. Smeared feces covered the wet concrete floor next to their upside-down water dish. The next kennel held an old, handsome, and distinguished brown-and-white springer spaniel. Sun-bleached beautiful blond curls spilled over his head. He shoved his paw under the door at me, his eyes pleaded with me to be let out.

I peered in the next kennel: a beautiful young yellow Lab like the one I'd grown up with balanced on three legs. His back leg hung sideways; it was obviously broken. Filled with horrible anxiety, I wondered, Had he been hit by a car? Was his owner looking for him? Although he wore a collar and tag, there was no information on the kennel. Would he be cleared out to make more room?

Salty snot ran onto my lips, and my face was cold and wet with tears from the intense pain that stabbed at my heart. This ugly prison was no place for innocent animals, or for a sensitive Cupcake like me. In that moment, my mind told me to try to stay tough.

I noticed an open door in the corner of the room and ran there to hide. In the dark room, my eyes and nose burned from the urine-soaked litter pans in the cages filled with cats and kittens. I was headed for a full meltdown if I didn't get out of that building soon. I was angry with myself for not bringing my crates that I used for my adoption days. It was time to move fast. Their lives now depended on me, and time was ticking away. For some odd reason, the thought of war came to me. It must have been all the M*A*S*H episodes I watched as a kid that taught me a commanding officer did his best to save all his men. People lived through wars and tremendous tragedies. It was time to cut off my emotions, be brave, and make every second count. That was what I had to do—save as many lives as possible.

With that specific mission in mind, I pushed my sunglasses down over my damp face, and walked back to the front desk.

Parker stood up, looked at me and asked, "Are you okay?"

Before I answered, the front door opened, and a middle-aged man walked in with an old, white poodle with cloudy eyes and an over-grown coat of curly, dirty fur. I heard the dog's untrimmed nails when they clicked against the tile floor. He said to Parker, "This was my mother's dog. She in a nursing home now, and we don't want him."

Parker looked annoyed and barked, "Well, we are plumb full. You might want to bring it back next week."

"No, we don't keep dogs. I'm leaving it here."

In a split second, my hand reached toward the man. I whispered, "Let me have him. I will find him a new home."

When I lifted the poodle into my car, he seemed to relax and quick-ly licked my face. I said, "You're not going in those kennels. You are coming home with me, baby boy."

Parker had followed me out. His chubby face grinned when he said in sweet tone, "At the rate you're going, you might want to get some crates." Then he pointed, "Head straight down this road, turn left at the light. Petco will be on your right. They got plenty of cages there. We don't have any, or I'd give them to ya." With sympathy in his voice, he continued, "Good thing you're taking those two dogs. When the owners surrender them to us, we walk them straight in the back for the vet. A stray animal might have an owner, so legally we have to hold them for seventy-two hours, unless they are in really bad shape."

I jumped in my SUV, and hurriedly shoved my hand through the window at him, "My name is Cupcake. I am pleased to meet you."

He said, "The name's Parker, and I am here to help."

When I pulled onto the road, my mind was instantly flooded with fear. In hopes of making a more specific plan and calming down, I spoke out loud to the border collie who was now sitting in my passenger seat. She stared at me as my hand ran slowly down her back, over and over. I said to her, "Okay, what the hell have I gotten myself into? Should I take the kittens? How many would they let me have? How many cages do I need?"

I would have another adoption event. But what about all the other animals in danger—where would they stay until I could organize another event? I looked at the border collie and gently squeezed her front paw, "Well, my new matted mess of a friend, you and Mr. Poodle will both get groomed at Petco while my new buddy Parker and I get more animals loaded for the freedom ride to Jackson Hole, Wyoming. You two are my first passengers, and you're both riding first class."

I leaned forward over the steering wheel and stopped at the red light. I exhaled with a sigh of relief; the border collie was safe in my car. Then I glanced back at the old poodle. His wet nose was twitching outside the open window; his ears blew back in the wind. A moment of clarity and peace washed over me.

The border collie was still staring at me as my blabber attack continued. "This appears to be my challenge, and this situation was given to me because I have some experience in finding new homes for orphaned animals. My plan right now is to buy as many crates as will fit into my car and take as many animals as possible."

I looked around my vehicle and sized up the space. I reached in the back of the car and put my hand under the poodle's chin and said "Oh, you don't know about my big mouth that normally gets me into trouble. Maybe that's not a curse, but a skill to be used when I tell everyone in Jackson what's going on over here."

By the time we arrived at Petco, my body was overtaken with nervous energy. In a state of complete anxiety inside the store, I called to a pimply-faced kid, "Get over here and help me." Without saying a word, he followed my orders, which only made me bossier. I hated to spend more money on crates, but thought, Well, this *was* supposed to be a shopping trip, not a raid on an animal shelter.

After the kid shoved the last crate in my car, I blurted out my final order, "Another thing you can do for me is to please get these two dogs groomed. Also buy them each a nice bone to chew on while they are waiting for their baths. Please make sure they get done ASAP." I gave him a handful of the twenty-dollar bills I had stuffed in my pocket for my shopping spree. "Oh, and please share that with the groomer. Thanks, kid, you're a real lifesaver, and I mean life saver. See you later today when I pick up the dogs."

Back at the shelter, a few officers stood behind the front counter and looked puzzled when I frantically tried to assemble the crates on the floor in front of them.

I grew angrier by the second, and burst out in a rude tone, "Are you going to charge me for the dogs and cats? They should be free if you're going to clean 'em out." Fully escalated, I snipped, "If you're just standing there and doing nothing, why don't you help me put these together?"

Parker knelt down, grabbed a metal crate, and snapped back, "Well, what the hell are you gonna do with all of them?"

Irritated, I said, "Find them good homes in Jackson. Isn't that what all of you are paid to do here?"

I went on and explained in more detail about my handful of mobile adoption events that had already placed a couple hundred cats and dogs.

Nervously, I asked again, "Are you going to charge for each animal I take?"

He grinned. "Well, for you I'd say they're free. Now that I know you're not gonna use them for target practice, take as many as you want. We got way too many coming in every day. I like to see them go out the front door, not the back. They'll all need to go to the vet for their shots, and most of them aren't fixed. And that ain't free either. You know, you seem like a real nice gal helping the Driggs shelter and now coming over here and taking some of ours."

Then I placed my hand on Parker's big shoulder and asked softly, "Will you please go pick out the other dogs and cats for me? Please bring me the springer spaniel."

He not only picked them out, but he also neatly stacked the crates and strapped them down inside my car, using every inch of room possible. He helped me load all the animals, and also told me there was a good, inexpensive vet just a block down the road. They spayed and neutered their animals after they were adopted. That clinic also boarded animals overnight for six dollars.

Within a year of my innocent but fateful stop at the Idaho Falls shelter, my credit card debt skyrocketed. The adoption fees I had charged for the cats and dogs did not cover my costs for amputations, spay or neuter surgeries, or to get them groomed. I worked three decent-paying jobs, never missed a payment, but teetered on the verge of bankruptcy.

Aside from being terrified by my mounting credit card debt, my thoughts were no longer on myself. Instead, my mind continuously plotted, planned, and obsessed about how to take more cats, kittens, dogs, and puppies out of that Idaho Falls shelter alive. All the animals in the Jackson shelter were safe; they were not killed to free up space. I even held a meeting at the Jackson shelter with the hope that they might be willing to help the animals in Idaho Falls. After everyone left, the manager followed me to the parking lot. "Quit bringing animals here. This is *my town*, and we don't need you or any of your rescues here."

Oh please, as if that would have stopped me! Her words only confirmed that I needed to start my own group. I envisioned a volunteer-run organization, and felt the animals needed as many people as possible to help them.

A Plan

Amy Vignaroli was a small pet-supply boutique owner in Jackson. We had spoken a few times about the possibility of sharing a space where the public could see and meet my foster animals. When Amy found a new location for her store, she called and asked me if I wanted the back half of the building for my orphans. With no savings, I hesitated, but something inside me knew this was the place, and I had to take it.

A kind, older woman had taken notice of my volunteer work for the shelter animals in Driggs. She had adopted two cats from one of my mobile adoption events where I had a large RV filled with cats; then, like a fairy godmother, she called me two days after Amy offered me the back store space. She wanted to give me a $50,000 gift to help my orphaned animals. But there was one major string attached: it had to be tax-deductible for her. This meant I had to start a nonprofit. I didn't know how to do that, but I called my friend Gregory Castle, one of the founders of Best Friends Animal Sanctuary in Kanab, Utah, for advice, and he put me through to their accountant. Then I wrangled my good friends Linda Osborne and Tom Patricelli under the guise of a two-for-one happy hour at the Cadillac Bar in Jackson. Our plans to open an adoption center for homeless animals began as scribbles on cocktail napkins.

When Dreams Become Reality

We held our grand opening for the Animal Adoption Center (AAC) in Jackson Hole, Wyoming, in March 2004. Our animal-loving town was ready to receive us, and eagerly dove in headfirst to help our animals.

Both locals and visiting tourists arrived by the hundreds, becoming foster parents, dog-walking volunteers, donors, and, of course, adopting animals we brought in from Driggs, Idaho Falls, and the surrounding area. Thousands upon thousands of unpaid working hours were devoted to our precious, cats, dogs, kittens, and puppies that were once slated for death in kill shelters. In less than the first four years of our operation, 1,280 animals were adopted in a town of 10,000 full-time residents. It was, and remains today, a phenomenal success.

This book begins with my childhood obsession with our family cat and moves on to tell the stories of my work volunteering for abandoned animals and founding the Animal Adoption Center. It shares a handful of uplifting animal rescue stories of seemingly impossible challenges overcome by the actions of loving people, and celebrates the wonderful, caring people who gave so much to bring about incredible outcomes. Entertaining and uplifting, this book sheds light on the solutions vital to saving the lives of homeless animals.

My hope and prayer is that you will be inspired and encouraged to join us in our mission so we may become a no-kill nation.

My Very First Num Num

Num Num

When I was a baby, my mother kept me in a foldout playpen in the kitchen while she worked. We had a beautiful, shiny black cat with golden almond-shaped eyes named Felix. The slightest glimpse of his black fur made me shriek with sheer excitement until my mother carried him to me. "Be gentle with our special kitty," she always told me. I would hold my breath, my eyes wide, and whisper, "Kee Cat, Kee Cat, Kee Cat." One day, my love for him overwhelmed me, and my little sausage-like fingers clenched slowly around his neck. In slow motion (so my mother wouldn't notice), I slowly leaned over him, and with my mouth open wide, my gums sank into the fur on his back. The muffled sound of "Num num num" drifted up faintly through his fur.

My mother was ready and quickly whisked him away from me and gently placed him in the warm sunshine on our couch. He casually licked my spit off his back and smoothed out his impeccably sleek fur, as if it were one of his daily baths. He pretended not to notice us. I know now that this is typical cat behavior: cool, nonchalant, and a bit self-righteous.

He had a few strands of drool on his fur but was otherwise fine. I, however, was a complete emotional wreck. Tears streamed down my pudgy pink cheeks, and snot bubbles boiled over in my crinkled-up nose. My lower lip, covered in his black fur, quivered as I sobbed, "Momma, num num. Momma, peeees! Kee Cat, Kee Cat." That was just one of the many times my mother knew I was different from most children.

Today my strange habit of making num num continues. You may as well know—all my animals also get daily little love bites when I wake up in the morning. Making num num on their backs is not enough for me anymore.

Introducing My Best Friend (MBF) Linda

In almost every story you are about to read, my best friend Linda was there. Being my best friend has not been easy, I am sure. Over the years, I would get wild, overemotional, have big ideas, and take on too much. Sometimes I accidentally blurted out of my mouth blunt, thoughtless, and careless remarks which unintentionally hurt people's feelings.

Linda Osborne and her rescue "Bonita" from Mexico

MBF Linda Anderson Osborne is Norwegian. She is six feet tall with shiny blond hair and soft, blue eyes, and always seems to wear a subtle expression of wisdom. Born in a family of real-life Vikings from Minnesota, her four giant brothers dwarf her (they all are over six-foot-five). But Linda has always held her own with them. And while we've never had a real fistfight or wrestled, she could beat me in a tussle, especially if I were laughing uncontrollably or happened to have a few drinks under my belt.

Over thirty years ago, Linda granted herself the authority to tell me to "back it down" whenever I am being impossible, irrational, or acting downright annoying. And it has always been her steady, level-headed thinking that helped me make sense of my jumbled thoughts. To this day, I appreciate every time she reined me in when no one else would have tried. Today, my life is better thanks to her critiquing and occasional scolding.

It was I, the naïve one, who made the first trip to the kill shelter and ended up with a house full of animals. It was I who had the unrelenting obsession to try to save them all (and I still do). Once Linda learned about how many animals were being killed, she immediately opened her heart—as well as her wallet and home—to a never-ending flow of homeless animals. Linda was not about to let them die if she could help save them. From that day on, we were joined at the hip, accompanied by a menagerie of orphaned dogs, puppies, cats, and kittens that took over our lives.

And, as mentioned earlier, it was over cocktails that I casually coerced Linda into helping me found the Animal Adoption Center. That was an overwhelming and daunting project that overtook every aspect of our existence for several years. It was difficult, heartbreaking, rewarding, and stressful all at the same time. During the first three years of operation, between the two of us—with our dedicated staff, hundreds of hardworking volunteers, and thanks to our generous donors—we took more than a thousand animals destined to die and placed them in loving homes. We raised adoptions in our area by forty percent.

When Linda and I would go to pull cats and dogs out of their cages at the kill shelter, her big blue eyes would well up with tears. She often said, "We are taking this one, too," or, "We have more room in the car and this one can sit on my lap," and, "My credit card is on file at the vet's office so we can board them there overnight and pick them up tomorrow." Linda never said, "We took too many animals." Linda never said, "We made a mistake."

Linda has always forgiven me when I needed forgiveness. When situations seemed hopeless, she always brought light and solutions. It was her calm, wise spirit and centeredness that built a strong foundation for our nonprofit. She was the brains of the operation and took no credit for the thousands of unpaid hours she worked. I am indebted to her. She is MBFF[1].

---

1   To anyone over the age of twenty, MBFF means my best friend forever.

Our perfect Trixie

The Dog of a Lifetime

In my early twenties, I ran a group home for intellectually challenged adults in Wisconsin. Working there, I saved money and planned my escape to Wyoming with two friends from college. Soon after I moved to Jackson, I met Olaf. We were at a dinner party, and I fell hopelessly in love with him. We started dating soon after.

From Germany originally, Olaf was born with a beautiful head of golden blond hair. He was five years old when his family immigrated to the United States for a better life. In his final year of high school, he began growing a thick blond beard, which over time became wild and long, resembling the mythical King Neptune. That beard, along with many other unique attributes, became his trademark. Built like a lowland gorilla, he looks like he might grunt, but his voice is sweet and gentle. As an adventurer, he made countless first descents in his kayak on uncharted rivers throughout the world: magazines and books about boating have referred to him as a real-life legend. Incredibly gifted with many talents of invention, he is a true Viking.

Walter, my cat at the time, was a beautiful black-and-tan short-haired tabby. He was a sickly little cat. After a dozen trips to the vet, Michael Dennis—the first vet I ever used for my pets—asked me if I wanted to trade my medical expenses for watching his two young boys. The barter system was—and still is—strong in our small town. Walter's constant medical needs had turned me into Michael's nanny. In addition to his two darling boys, he had two exceptional border col-lie-Australian shepherd mixes, and he told me the combination of the two breeds made them the smartest dogs in the world. Michael was a real showoff when it came to their tricks. Fred, the younger dog, knew about thirty words, and his older one, Sam, was the Einstein of the two, with a sixty-word vocabulary. While I enjoyed his two adorable sons, Sam and Fred were my preferred company.

Fred and Sam seemed to understand everything I said when I spoke to them. Okay, maybe it was my imagination, but they actually seemed interested when I engaged in what my brother calls blabber attacks. I'd go on and on, telling them all about my boring life. These so-called "cow dogs" were bred to work livestock, cows, or sheep. They are also referred to as herding dogs or working dogs. I learned later that relationships with these animals are based on mutual respect with unsaid words. They sit by your side and are bred to take commands, work, and please their person. It's truly a magical connection.

New to Wyoming, I was as-yet unaware that this type of loyal dog was the preferred breed out west. Cow-dog people regularly stopped me to admire Michael's gorgeous four-legged boys. Of course, I proudly pretended they were mine. I was happy to return Michael's kids, but when Fred and Sam jumped into his truck, my heart hurt. Several times I said I wanted one of my own. Then, a friend called and asked me to find a home for a small border collie puppy from her neighbor who was a rancher.

We met at a gas station. He pulled the pup out of a box and said she was the last of the bunch. He had owned her mama, a little border collie named Jo-Jo. The little pup's daddy was a blue merle Australian shepherd who had taken a bullet after he'd chased a neighbor's sheep one too many times. The litter was born on Christmas Day in 1999 and he said her mother was the smartest working dog in their county.

This little pup had a big, white skunk stripe down the middle of her face. She was incredibly beautiful and also quite clever. I knew finding her a home would be easy, and that Olaf and I would have some fun playing with her until she was adopted. I did not own my own home at that time, and was not about to get a dog until I did.

Olaf's home had slowly turned into a dog kennel once I started volunteering and fostering with the shelter in Driggs, Idaho. He often complained when a new cat or a dog suddenly appeared in his living room or in his bed. As I drove back to the ranch with the stunning puppy in my lap, for a split second I worried whether this puppy would be the one to finally push him over the edge.

Olaf was gathering tools from the shop when he spotted the puppy's head as she peered out of the top of my coat. His kind blue eyes softened when he grabbed the irresistible puppy from me and said, "Looks like you're packing a puppy there. Now that is one good-looking baby skunk."

I responded, "Don't call her a skunk. Her name is Trixie." Another request ignored; her nickname Skunk stuck.

For most of his life, Olaf had worked on the ranch of a former governor and senator of Wyoming, and he preferred to work alone on his projects. As a physically strong individual with his own ideas, coworkers or anyone who tried to boss him around only aggravated him—including dogs. So, I was surprised when, shortly after meeting Trixie, he emerged from the house with a cup of coffee in his hand and the gorgeous puppy under his muscular arm. He said, "Let's get back to work." He wasn't angry—he was smitten. After just two minutes, Olaf had taken the puppy from me and had gone to work with her! At the time, I didn't know placing a puppy with a foster parent wasn't a good idea. Foster failure is most likely to occur with puppies or kittens. But it never crossed my mind that my bullheaded boyfriend would succumb to failure. Failure was something he did not do.

Skunk regularly swept the fields of the Canada geese. She waded into the irrigation ditches to herd the suckerfish. Her daddy taught her how to crack open pistachios and eat only the nut. She learned to drink from a straw and, when given a hamburger, she'd carefully pick off all the onions one by one. Olaf said she was a working skunk, and she should work to have her hamburger the way she liked it. A week after he'd made her his beloved coworker, he was getting ready for work one morning when I said, "Leave Trixie here. She needs to find her forever home, and I'm taking her into town today to meet a few people who are interested in her. We're not keeping her. I won't have a dog when I don't own my own house."

On his way out the door, he picked her up and laughed. "Don't worry, Skunk-momma. We are keeping her." Yet another of my requests that had fallen on deaf ears. That was it—Trixie was our dog. Olaf had failed as a foster parent.

An old ranch hand named Roy Martin worked on the ranch where Olaf and I lived with Trixie. He had rough-looking teeth, thick, scratched glasses, and a skinny, stiff little body. He always had a pinch of tobacco wedged under his lower lip, and a stain from the brown spit that seeped out of the corner of his mouth. He had noticed our new precious baby and gave me some solid, old-school advice. "Now you listen here, young lady. You never raise a hand to a border collie. Just raise your voice and that will do. If you raise a hand to them, you'll ruin them. They aim to please. They are not hardheaded. There's nothing in this world as satisfying as having a dog like this by your side." That sounded great to me since Olaf was hardheaded and took no demands, let alone polite requests. He was stubborn, and things usually had to be his way. When Olaf left the gates open and the cows tried to get out, Skunk barked and pushed them back. She also took a few rides down the Snake River on the deck of Olaf's kayak as he proudly paddled his most prized possession, his baby Skunk.

Just like old, crusty darling Roy had once said, true to the border collie nature, Skunk was one sensitive girl. If someone yelled on TV, she would get upset and sit on our feet, with her ears pinned to her head. If a gun went off in the distance, she'd tremble and look to us for some sort of explanation. Roy's advice was straight on, except that if we had raised our voices to Skunk it would have destroyed her. A look of disappointment and a headshake was all it took, especially from her loving daddy, whom she idolized.

After she was spayed, Olaf heard her whimper and carried her outside to do her business. I spied on them through the bathroom window and eavesdropped as he reassured her with baby talk. "Now, your mommy did that to you, not me. You're going to be all right. I'm sorry if it hurts." In the thirteen years we'd spent together, I'd never heard him use a baby voice, apologize to a dog, or insist on taking one with him everywhere he went. With Skunk at his side, he was a different person altogether. His face lit up when he told me about their day at work. He had finally found a coworker that he not only liked but deeply adored. He was her teacher, her master, and her protective father. She was his baby and his friend who wisely never told him what to do.

In the mornings, right before leaving, he'd say, "Skunk, let's go to work." When the front door opened, she'd run to the truck, backhoe, or the dirt bike. Olaf would point to the machine and give her the command to load up. She'd climb into the cab of the backhoe, jump through the window of his truck, or carefully balance herself on the seat of his dirt bike, and off they'd go.

Trixie wanted to work. After all, cow dogs need a job, and hers was to keep her daddy happy while she kept the geese, fish, and cows in their place.

When Skunk was still a baby, she was pouncing on mice in the pasture while Olaf was digging with the backhoe. A couple of coyotes had snuck behind her; they yipped and barked. It was a sly, cunning invitation for her to come and play. Her protective father called her back and put her safely in the cab, then looked her in the eye and told her in a serious, low tone that those were bad dogs. Any time Olaf saw a coyote, he'd point to them and say, "Skunk, there's a bad dog." She'd growl and carry on as he reminded her that coyotes like the taste of skunk, especially baby skunk, because it's quite tender and juicy. Olaf deserved half the credit for Skunk's unbelievable skills. She had the intelligence but needed his direction. He schooled her on hundreds of acres of open ranch land, many times tucked caringly under his muscular arm, pressed close to his big chest.

One day when they were in the old ranch dump truck, Olaf punched the gearshift into place. Skunk groaned at the grinding noise, put her paw on Olaf's shoulder, and looked at him with concern. He later asked me, "How does she know what the transmission of the truck should sound like?" I didn't know. Somehow, she did.

And one night, while I watched the evening news, a tragic story brought me to tears. Skunk climbed on top of me and cautiously put her eye next to mine, and then her nostril next to my nostril. (This became known as the border collie body scan.) She licked my tears and stayed on me until my tears subsided.

Under her diligent watch one morning, Trixie pressed her eye next to mine, groaned and licked my face until she got me out of bed. This was no body scan—something was wrong. She ran to the sliding glass door and barked viciously. I asked, "Is it a bad dog?"

Her high-pitched bark shot through my head like a bullet. She gently pulled on my nightgown with her teeth until we stood in front of the sliding glass door. There sat a large brown bear at our picnic table; his tightly clenched paws held the grill that was covered in charred salmon skin. She knew he was not welcome. I told her, "Well, now, that was my mistake." She barked at the bear through the glass until he ran off. And then I thoroughly cleaned the dirty grill and locked it tightly in the shed. Skunk ate scrambled eggs with ham and cheese for breakfast and was given lots of extra kisses that morning. Her warning reminded me to never accidently attract bears, as it does not end well for them. Out here, a fed bear is a dead bear.

Over the years, one of my many jobs has been to care for elderly people in their homes. Trixie went with me on all my jobs. At one of my client's, I slept with a baby monitor next to the bed in case the patient needed assistance. If anyone stirred more than Dr. Skunk thought was normal, she'd sprint into their bedroom, give them a quick body scan, and then run back to me and push me hard enough to fall out of bed and onto the floor.

One night I stumbled into the bedroom of a little ninety-two-year-old ranch lady. I stood in a stupor by her bed when she yelled, "Where the hell you been? The dog's been in here twice now." I never worried about sleeping too hard. Dr. Skunk handled the night shift for me.

It was at the same house when Trixie stuck her head into the shower and moaned until I followed her downstairs, wrapped in a towel. The client's cats had tipped over a vase of flowers on the table. A small pool of water had slowly dripped onto the carpet. Not a real tragedy, but she knew something was not right. How did she know that water damages the finish on tables?

Years later, on an especially frigid night (twenty degrees below zero), our dogs ran out for a quick last call. Trixie followed close behind my older, deaf cow dog, Henry Thomas, as I stood on the porch and shivered in my robe with chattering teeth. A small mountain of snow had piled up in the driveway from the plow. Standing behind it was an enormous bull moose. When the dogs got too close, he sauntered into the light from the porch with his ears angrily flattened back; his hackles were up. Then he charged Henry Thomas from behind. Skunk darted in and nipped at the fifteen-hundred-pound animal's heels as he tried in vain to kick Henry Thomas. She circled him and barked until he ran off, without a doubt saving Henry from getting stomped to death.

Skunk squealed on many foster dogs when they chewed the wrong things or chased my cats. Normally I don't like squealers, but her warnings were warranted, and greatly appreciated. Under her care, she kept the junk show of my life together. She used to wake me up if a cat or dog had gotten sick in the middle of the night. When the cats tried to shred the couch, she gently pushed them off with her nose. If woodpeckers pecked on our house, she barked at them until they flew away. She saved people, carpeting, furniture, the siding of our house, and kept me gainfully employed when she worked the night shift.

Most of all, she protected and comforted me when I was sick. And when I fell into a deep well of depression, she was the only one who was able to pull me out. My wish for my own cow dog came true when I agreed to foster her. In return, her daddy and I were rewarded with the greatest gift of a lifetime. Olaf and I had thirteen years of a wild, fun-filled, crazy romance. Trixie was the dog of a lifetime, and Olaf was the love of my life.

Harvey

Helping Harvey

Like millions of animals in our country, Harvey had been dumped at a shelter. He was an older, blond cocker spaniel, and not only was he terribly overweight, Harvey also had a serious limp. As if that wasn't bad enough, the poor guy also suffered from a terrible medical condition that left him mostly bald with huge patches of bumpy, purple skin.

I met Harvey on one of my trips to the Driggs shelter and was worried about him. When I called the shelter manager and asked to foster him, her response was, "We're not sure if we're going to put him down. He had a stroke after you left."

About four months after my request to foster Harvey, I called the same shelter to discuss my Christmas mobile adoption event in Jackson. The shelter manager said, "Hey, I still have that old cocker if you want me to bring him."

I'd forgotten about Harvey and felt sick with guilt. "Oh God, yes, of course, you must bring him." There was no way he'd be overlooked at the adoption event. I knew if I tried hard enough, someone would take him home that night.

Mobile adoption events are generally tents or booths set up in a high-traffic location to make the animals more accessible for the public to meet and greet. We advertised our mobile adoption event for a month on the radio, the local TV station, and in the newspaper. To pay for the advertising, we rented booths to vendors to sell crafts, Christmas trees, and wreaths. We hoped to bring in more traffic—higher adoption numbers—and thus more foster parents.

Leading up to the adoption event, my friends and I donned elf boots and elf ears with matching hats and handed out invitations to people on the street. We teased those we knew that either they come peacefully, or I'd do a Tony-Soprano-style drive-by adoption and drop off dogs and cats at their houses on our way home. My heart knew no animal should have to sit behind bars, especially at Christmas, a time when we think of the less fortunate, especially orphans without a home.

At the time of our event, Harvey had been at the Driggs shelter for more than six months. Where he was bald on his back, he'd grown a hump of blubber. He had a beautiful, kind, loving face, but looked like the Hunchback of Notre Dame. The stroke had left his face partially paralyzed, and a thyroid condition had made his skin a complete mess that was painful to look at. Poor Harvey looked like he had been burned with a flamethrower. He wore a new, tight red wool sweater that was stretched over his blubber, which kept him warm and covered his hideous skin. We also added a small plastic wreath to his collar and put angel wings on his back in a lame attempt to disguise his physical deformities.

No outfit could have hidden all his conditions, but no animal or person was happier to be at the adoption party than Harvey. I told him he needed to mind his manners if he wanted to find a home. God knows Harvey needed all the help he could get. Anyone who didn't immediately wince when they saw him was an invitation I took, and I'd hand them his leash with a request to take him for a quick walk.

Upon their return, I'd ask if they would please foster Harvey for the night. He was obviously quite happy and loveable, but his medical conditions made people apprehensive. Harvey looked like he had one paw in the grave and another on a banana peel. I got it—no one wanted to fall in love with him and quickly end up with a broken heart.

When the night drew to an end, he had not found a foster home. I whispered in his ear that he would not return to the shelter and that the party had been thrown for him. He was so gullible, he believed me. Harvey had run from person to person all night long and wagged his nub of a tail until I thought it would fall off.

Thanks to everyone involved, our Home 4 the Holidays event was a huge success. We had a great turnout, with several hundred people attending and a whopping seventy-four adoptions! We also made the front page of the local newspaper. There were many more people interested in adopting, but they each had to check with their spouses, roommates, or landlords before they committed. We fostered out—and also boarded at the vet—a total of twenty-five animals overnight, and all of them were ultimately adopted or sent to foster homes!

It was the end of our busy night. Harvey lay dead asleep in the middle of the floor with his spit-covered rubber pork chop tucked under his head as if it were a pillow. His party was over. Every person in the room had been asked to foster him, but no one took him home.

The Driggs shelter manager approached me and said, "We're all loaded up. You're taking him, right? Maybe you can get him adopted—that is, if he doesn't have another stroke and die."

Harvey had to either come home with me, go back to the shelter, or be boarded at the vet. I'd promised him he would not live behind bars again. I shook my head, started my truck, turned on the heat, and cleared a spot for him. Maybe the party really had been for him? After all, he was going to a home, just not the one I'd planned.

Carrying Harvey was like carrying a sixty-pound sack of potatoes. He barely moved as he plopped down on the front seat of my truck wrapped in my goose-down jacket. As we drove home, I gently rubbed his head and felt genuine holiday joy for the cats and dogs that had been taken to their new homes. I told myself, If Harvey has another stroke and dies at my house in a soft warm bed with his slimy rubber pork chop and my little, striped cat Frida as his nurse, it would be better than dying alone on a cold concrete floor in a crummy blanket.

He had such a great time at his party that he barely moved the next morning. It took a few days for him to regain his strength, but Harvey lived—and let me tell you, he lived like he never had before.

At the time, I had three jobs and three dogs. I begged my friends to help me foster Harvey, and they did. Altogether, he had five foster homes. Our love for him formed a huge extended family that adored our half-dead cocker spaniel. He went from house to house with his little suitcase of toys, diet food, medication, and of course, his rubber pork chop, wearing his extra-large, new, red sweater that barely fit around his enormous girth.

He cross-country skied with us, rode on snowmobiles, and took daily walks in his red wool cable sweater as he flung his stiff front leg out in front of him. With the combination of his soaked diet food, thyroid pills, and intense exercise program, Harvey lost twenty-five pounds and his hump of blubber in just three months! His bald spot grew into silky beautiful waves of shiny golden fur.

Although his face still drooped and his front leg never really bent normally again, Harvey's paw never landed on a banana peel. He settled happily into the lives of his adoring foster families.

Eight months later, my brother, mother, and cousins from Colorado came to town to help me with a fundraising event for homeless animals. Loud, crazy animal lovers filled my house. Harvey was beside himself. He ran from one person to the next. He squeaked his pork chop and furiously wiggled his nubby tail. He probably thought we'd planned the family reunion just for him. After all, he liked to party, and he was the center of attention. His joyful, silly demeanor made everyone happy because his enthusiasm for life was so contagious.

My cousin Heather from Colorado had come up for the event and thought Harvey was perfect; she wanted to take him home. Her husband Robert was from England. He fancied border collies and had said that someday, when they lived in the country, they'd get one. He quietly told my cousin, "He is way too old. You will be devastated when he dies." Robert had made up his mind, and the answer was no.

But Robert didn't realize that "no" does not mean no to our family. Heather had made up her mind that Harvey was going home with them. The night before they left, my aunt, Heather's mother, told Robert that Harvey had found a home in Colorado. She said the three of them would drop him off there on their way home.

I didn't look Robert in the eyes when we said goodbye. Instead, I sobbed and tried to catch my breath as Harvey drove away in their car.

After eight months together it was going to be hard for me to live without him. My only consolation was that Heather had him and knew how special he was. He remained safely tucked within my family.

My time with him was over. The wait for a good home had been worth it for me and especially for him. His time with us in Jackson had enriched the lives of those of us who had fostered him.

Heather drove home with my aunt in the passenger seat. They were halfway through Colorado when Robert awoke from his nap. He looked at Harvey and said, "You both lied to me! He's coming home to live with us, isn't he?" Robert refused to speak for the rest of the trip or to allow Harvey to sit next to him. He sat in the back seat with his arms crossed tightly over his chest and looked angry as he stared out the window.

My aunt whispered to Heather, "Well, I said we would drop him off at his new home. He just didn't know it was your home." Harvey had found his new family, but not the one Robert had planned.

A week after they returned home, Robert became extremely sick. He was too weak to resist Harvey when he climbed into bed with him. Robert had come down with the West Nile virus.

Harvey refused to leave him, apart from quick potty breaks. As Robert slowly began to heal, the two became inseparable. Robert nicknamed him "Sir Stubbs," for his nubby tail, and proudly referred to himself as his father. Heather said she wasn't sure who loved whom more.

Sir Stubbs's reign as the Ambassador of Goodwill continued in Colorado. He worked at a nursing home with his mother, Heather. People regularly requested Harvey's presence for children's birthday parties, neighborhood cookouts, and sleepovers for nieces and nephews. I teased Heather and Robert, "Harvey should run for mayor. With a following like his, he's sure to win."

Who knew that a half-dead, homeless cocker spaniel with a caved-in face and stiff front leg would touch people's lives and hearts the way Harvey did? I sure didn't. But I do know that as we cared for him, he made us better people.

Making Your Voice Heard

The first few months at the Animal Adoption Center were incredibly exciting. It was like a wild, nonstop party. We were slammed with hundreds of visitors and made big weekly pulls from the neighboring kill shelter in Idaho Falls. John Parker had become one of our favorite characters. We used a deep silly voice when we called him "Parker!" And in his gruff voice he called each of us "darlin'." He was a big teddy in a blue polyester uniform who liked to tell bad jokes and act goofy with us. Most importantly, he went out of his way to help us save their animals.

We had been open for about five months when he called me for help. His voice sounded strained when he said, "Well, darlin', the wall on the decompression chamber has caved in, so it can't be used. The shelter's packed to the roof with dogs and cats. The dog kennels that normally hold one dog now have three or four dogs crammed into them. I was hoping that you and your people would come over and help us out."

Flabbergasted, I thought, A decompression chamber? At the time, I knew they killed for room at least once a week but was unaware of how they did it.

I yelled, "Please, Parker, cancel the vet. We'll be there early tomorrow morning!"

Parker said, "Now listen, darlin', you have no idea how many animals we've got. I'll put him off till eleven, which will give you some time. I'm going to tell you right now, you won't be able to take them all."

Heather, my office manager at the time, was perfect in almost every respect, but had a fearful disposition and nervously tracked our bank balance every day of the week. And rightly so, as we were broke every other week. She said, "Now, Cupcake, I know we need more cats and dogs, but we simply can't afford it right now. We don't have the money now to pay all the bills we owe. Pulling more animals would be a big financial mistake."

Heather was always right, the voice of reason. I needed her and Linda to keep me in line. But I was the boss and was distinctly remembering Nathan Winograd's speech at the Best Friends Animal Society conference where he shared how he took the Thompkins County Animal Shelter in Ithaca, New York, to no-kill, literally overnight. He used the media and asked for help on TV. I knew the time had come for me to take similar actions.

My mind was made up. We were going to get those animals no matter how much she warned me not to. I told her, "It will work out. They are not killing these animals if we can pull them. It's time everyone in our community knows what goes on behind closed doors at that shelter. We live in a great town, with loving people, and they will help us save them if we ask. I am going to ask with a radio commercial." Before the prevalence of cell phones and the internet, people listened to the local Jackson radio station. Within thirty minutes after Parker's call, I had recorded a one-minute radio commercial for $100. It would air the next day every thirty minutes. Everyone in our town would hear my cry for help.

Then it was time to round up volunteers. My only real requirement was that they have a big SUV full of gas and could take orders. Our rock-star volunteers at the Center—the eleven-year-old, strong and capable Amanda Gates; and the ten-year-old, intelligent and calculating Krystal Hoffman—had done countless runs to the Idaho Falls shelter. They knew the inside of that building, the staff, and how to get into the back room where they killed the animals. Skilled, serious, and unmatched at handling dogs and people, they had also trained our new volunteers, both young and old. They were the perfect choice to help us take charge of the inexperienced adult volunteers on this run. Linda, Parker, Krissi Goetz—our brilliant media manager, and I ran where we were needed while we supervised the operation, keeping it safe and organized as best as we could.

There was a large vet clinic a block away from that shelter where we regularly boarded, treated, and fixed the animals we pulled. I paid that vet's office not when we dropped them off, but when we picked them up. That bought me time to raise the money to pay them.

After a sleepless night and a few too many cocktails, I got up the next morning while it was still cool, and the air was damp. I jumped into a friend's large passenger van, turned the ignition, and turned on the radio just as my voice came on the air. As I listened to my plea, I began to panic about how many animals we needed to take, where they would all go, and how many would fit in our vehicles. I also knew there would be some that we would be forced to leave behind. My stomach felt a pang of nausea, and my eyes were tired and burned. But within minutes of our first commercial airing, Heather called me to say our phones were ringing off the hook at the AAC.

It was early in the morning when we loaded eight adult volunteers and dozens of crates into six big SUVs and the big white passenger van I had borrowed. The van would be used to transport the cats back to Jackson. Our cars formed a long line; the kids and I were in the front. I jumped out and screamed to the drivers, "Are you ready to make the biggest pull in the history of the AAC? I say, yes! Let's hit it!"

When we arrived at the shelter, all the volunteers formed a circle outside and I handed out earplugs and said in a loud voice, "Leave your emotions out here." We wrapped our arms around each other's shoulders and leaned in, and then I said, "When we're inside, you need to focus and do exactly what the girls, Linda, Krissy, and I tell you to do."

I saw Olaf's face in my mind when I said, "No crying; save it for later. We must move quickly and not waste one single second. The veterinarian will be here to euthanize the cats and dogs in less than two hours. We have plenty of time if we move efficiently and carefully." I added, "Now, Dear God and Good Forces that Be, help us get as many animals out of here as possible today!" We then broke like a football team from a huddle and entered the unusually crowed front room, bearing leashes around our necks and flip phones tucked into our pockets.

When Parker saw me, he yelled from behind the front desk, "Hey, darlin', I knew you'd come! Looks like you found some friends to help. Now you go ahead and take as many as you're able. You better hurry up. The vet will be here shortly."

In front of the counter, a line of irate people who wanted to surrender their animals was building. Parker yelled to the crowd, "Please keep your animal at home! We're full, and I mean we have no damn room anywhere in this building!"

Single file, we entered the big dog room. I flinched, confronted with the horrid, humid stench as the shrill barking penetrated my foam earplugs. Each kennel had more than three dogs crammed into it. Desperate to get free, the dogs wailed, shrieked, and jumped up and down on each other, covered in their own filth. Without the earplugs, the high-pitched barking would have been deafening. It must have been a nightmare for the animals. I looked each frightened volunteer in the eye and yelled over the dogs, "Be brave! We can do this!"

Our team leaders ran into their places and quickly leashed the dogs, while our dog wrangler Amanda did runs to the backyard with up to five leashed dogs at a time. She was young, strong, fast, and also pretty tricky.

Within the hour, the backyard was overflowing with beautiful dogs of every size, breed, and color. They settled down after they relieved themselves, sniffed each other, and marked the grass. Linda and I patted down the dogs for possible tumors, pregnancy, infected gums, broken teeth, injuries, or open wounds. We stayed close to them and grabbed their leashes if it looked as though a fight may occur. We were about ninety minutes into our triage when a big truck pulled up in the parking lot. Amanda recognized the truck and shouted, "Cuppers, the vet's here! He's early! Now what do we do?"

I yelled, "Go to the back room!"

Amanda suddenly cocked her head and said, "Don't worry, Cuppers. We got this one. Come on, Krystal!"

Like a couple of highly trained Navy SEALs, Krystal and Amanda took charge and ran to the side door and into the back room where, with Parker in tow, they locked the doors and Amanda pushed a chair up under the doorknob.

This particular vet was known to be short-tempered and, to put it nicely, let's just say he was unpopular, especially with the shelter staff in Idaho who often complained to me that they couldn't stand his rude demeanor or his ill-mannered wife who helped him euthanize the animals. Good old Doc Pierre. Thanks to our young, skilled SEALs on their mission, it took more than twenty minutes before he was finally able gain access to the back room. I was in the back of the shelter when I heard him yell, "Where are all of the dogs? You said you were full! I didn't come over here for nothing!"

I wondered why he'd come an hour early, and if he got paid for each animal he euthanized. I laughed and said under my breath, "Well, Mr. Popular and Mr. Over-Punctual, looks like you have been outsmarted by a ten- and an eleven-year-old today." Before Doc Pierre could get into the back, Parker had pulled the van around to the back door of the shelter and helped the girls load it full of dogs, which included two huge totes filled with puppies and their nursing mothers. They were taken to the vet—only three blocks from the shelter—where they were boarded, fixed, vaccinated, and quarantined. The back room had been emptied, except for a few chickens someone had surrendered.

Behind the shelter, things were turning into a three-ring circus. In an effort to maintain safety, I monitored the young dogs and volunteers, and wondered where the other shelter staff were. That's when I looked in the office window and saw two chubby officers stuffing donuts in their faces as they laughed. They were obviously not planning on helping us load the animals. Filled with overpowering rage, I stomped into the office, threw a dog collar on the floor, and screamed, "Did you forget that you get paid to help them? Not kill them. Why in the hell aren't you helping us?"

They dropped their donuts, hung their heads, followed me outside, and started loading the dogs. Parker came out and whispered to me, "I helped your little gals in the back room. The vet is madder than hell. They are really something. We got them all out before he could get in there! How many are you gonna take today?"

My hackles were up, and I shouted, "As many as your lazy officers can help me pack into our vehicles! Now, where are my cats? I've got a huge van for them to ride in; give me as many as you've got. We have to hurry before our favorite vet gets in the cat room!"

Parker apologized and said, "We've never seen anything like it before. My boys counted more than forty dogs loose in the back, and not one fight. Some of your friends even tied a few dogs to the trees."

I said, "I told them to, so they'd be safe from Doc Pierre."

All our crates were being used for the dogs; we had run out. The two shamed animal control officers with powdered sugar on their lips carried the cats out to the van in pillowcases. Yes, *pillowcases*! It was terrifying to see them wriggling in the large cotton sacks. One of the officers told me they did this all the time when someone adopted a cat, and that they'd be okay if it was a short ride. The cats in the cases were handed to me through the van window, and once inside, the cats were immediately let free of their sacks. Like I said, we didn't go over there for nothing!

Without much sleep and slightly hungover, a dull pain pulsed behind my tired red eyes. The drive home would be a time to rest, and in my exhaustion, I dreaded the amount of work it would take to get all our precious cargo settled. I rested my head on the steering wheel while dozens of loose cats found their places on or under the vinyl seat benches. They occasionally swatted at each other, hissed, and growled.

The new volunteers looked anxious sitting in their cars, but Amanda and Krystal were beaming. I signaled for Amanda to join me in the van and act as a referee for the confused, frightened cats. She jumped in and said, "Wait till you hear this, Cuppers. I watched this scary detective show last night where this guy was being chased by a murderer. But he saved himself when he jammed a chair under the doorknob and the killer was locked out!"

I said, "What? It was no mistake you saw that, sister! Do you know how proud I am of you and Krystal today, running the show and getting all the dogs out of the back room? I mean, you two are unbelievable gifts from heaven. We never could have done it without you and Krystal—never! Remind me to get Parker a nice present next week. Now help me stay awake. I'm beyond tired and need a double espresso, but no one in Idaho knows what espresso is, so you may need to slap me to keep me awake in our newly converted cat van. Wait till the girls in the office see all these beautiful animals! This morning was unbelievable. We've got one heck of a team. You and Krystal are the most valuable team members. I love you, Amanda."

Amanda said, "I think this is the best day of my life so far."

I nodded and smeared a tear off my face with my wrist and said, "Me too, baby girl, me too."

Then I turned around and told the cats, "Listen up! I'm sorry and quite frankly shocked that you were put in pillowcases today. That was a new one on me, and it will never happen again. You are all safe and going to my big garage until we can get you to a vet and find each of you a fantastic new home. So, sit back and enjoy the ride. Our final destination today is Jackson, Wyoming, my lucky feline friends. Oh and no fighting please; don't make me pull over and turn into my dad."

Heather had called my cell phone several times. Amanda listened to the messages. The office was apparently full of anxious people waiting for the animals to arrive. She also wanted to know how many animals we had taken. But I did not answer her calls. I knew what she'd say. She might even quit when we pulled up with six vehicles packed full of dogs and a van filled with over a dozen uncrated cats. I was too tired and weak to care; it was done, and they were safe with us for now. We had emptied more than half of the animals out of the shelter.

Amanda said, "Oh boy, Heather is going to be really mad at you. We have quadrupled our normal numbers, not including all the ones boarding at the vet. Let's tell her about those next week once she's cooled off."

I said, "You're right. Good thinking, Ms. Smarty Pants. Grab the wheel if I drift off the road. You're the copilot and I shouldn't be driving."

By the time we returned to the adoption center in Jackson, my eyes itched uncontrollably and were almost swollen shut from exhaustion and tears—and cat allergy, one I didn't realize I had until after driving hours with a vanful of cats. We pulled into the parking lot to find every single space taken. I was crabby and said, "Who are all of these people parked here on such a hot, beautiful summer day? Why aren't they out having fun?" It was a blistering ninety degrees, but the hair stood up on my arms when I realized the lot was full of our new volunteers. Then I saw Heather. She was surrounded by a sea of people in a grassy vacant lot behind the Center. I anticipated a serious lecture, or maybe her resignation, and covered my eyes with my hands and put my head down again on the steering wheel.

Amanda quickly jumped out and said, "Good luck, Cuppers!"

Heather walked up to the van with her clipboard resting on her hip. Her tone was sharper than usual. "Okay, Cupcake, we've had a lot of donations. I'm not sure of the total amount yet, but it's well into the thousands. At least fifty people are doing various volunteer jobs we created. They're ready to wash dogs and whatever else needs to be done, and your garage has been remodeled into a swanky big cat house. This day has been absolutely insane. The Center is jammed so full of visitors that no one can move in the office. Both phone lines have been ringing nonstop all day long!"

Heather never complained, and she never said we made a mistake. She continued, "This day has been a real-life miracle; I mean, an honest-to-God miracle! It's hard to believe all these people coming out of the woodwork to help."

I watched her as she walked over to each vehicle and tagged the animals as they were unloaded. She wiped her eyes several times with her sleeve.

I entered the building and began wading slowly through the back hallway, which was jammed shoulder to shoulder with men, women, and kids of all ages. Some people handed me personal checks, cash, and credit cards. Kids held bags of dog treats or handfuls of change. They shook my hand and patted my back. Strangers asked to hug me while thanking us for getting the animals to Jackson. Brand-new bags of dog food and toys were piled in the four corners of the room. Then I suddenly realized they had all been waiting for me, the voice on the radio. I snapped out of my exhaustion and felt alert. My eyes overflowed with love for the people, and I hugged the kids who held out sweaty coins and dog treats.

The large office clock on the wall read 3:00 p.m. It had been exactly twenty-four hours since Parker's call came in for our help. The dogs they couldn't kill fast enough were now being bathed by volunteers. All the cats that would have never made it out the front door of that shelter were being chauffeured to a large, comfortable penthouse formerly known as my garage. I felt a huge wave of relief pass through my body. This was working out. No mistake had been made.

Almost all the animals that day were adopted by their foster parents or by the homes they found with their friends, relatives, neighbors, or coworkers. We gathered dozens of new adopters, foster parents, volunteers, and donors who supported our mission. They were eager to give their love and provide aid to our precious cats, dogs, and adorable kittens and puppies.

It's important to mention that we were extremely fortunate that none of the animals had any contagious diseases or aggression issues. That alone was a miracle. Living at a high elevation with nine months of freezing weather means that animals don't get most of the diseases found in the South, like heartworm, fleas, ticks, or distemper. The incredibly generous donations from our fellow animal-loving and concerned citizens paid the entirety of the bills, and left us with a good nest egg, finally giving Heather a well-deserved break from worrying.

We had asked people for their help, and they showed up with loving hearts in great numbers, eager to be part of this mission. Our overwhelming successes came from working together as a team. The best news of all is that, thankfully, that shelter in Idaho Falls, and thousands like it, no longer kill for space.

Cofounder Linda Osborne

Volunteer Krystal

Volunteer Amanda Gates

Media Manager Krissy Goetz

Volunteer Sierra

Our Secret Weapons

Rays of bright sunlight illuminated the billows of cigar smoke that slowly swirled around him. His thick black hair was combed back with shiny grease. His overly tanned brown face was covered with deep gashes of wrinkles. He held a crystal glass that twinkled in the rays of light through the gold whiskey. He spoke out of the side of his mouth, and his voice sounded like he had gravel in his throat. He was no blood relation to me; he was married to my grandmother's sister. He was our uncle Russ.

It was on my first visit to Uncle Russ's house in the early 1970s when he ordered my brother, sister, and me into his golf cart and punched the gas pedal to the floor. Our heads shot backward, and our feet flung straight into the air. Like a wild ride at the fair, we squealed with exhilaration. In that moment, I knew he liked to have fun even though, in my eyes, he was old.

Uncle Russ had a small private golf course on his farm. He slammed on the brakes at the edge of his driving range and ordered, "Come up one by one and introduce yourself to me so I know who you are." I jumped in front of him and quickly thrust my hand out toward his.

He crushed my tiny grip with his huge, leathery, baseball mitt of a hand, and then took a short sip of whiskey and a long drag from his cigar. Out of the side of his mouth with his gravelly voice, he said slowly, "Well, you little brat, is that all ya got for me?" He then told my brother, sister, and me that we were all brats. He said we would be referred to as brats until we could prove ourselves otherwise.

"Now you all listen up. If you're going to spend time with me, I need to know what you got." And looking at me, he said, "That, my dear, is not a real handshake. I know you can do better." His challenging words were ones I took seriously, so I gritted my teeth and grabbed his large hand. I scrunched up my face and tried to crush it with all my strength.

He leaned back and smiled, "Now that's better; you're my kind of kid. Go grab a club, and I'll show you three brats how it's done."

For the next hour, he proceeded to instruct the three of us on how to hit a golf ball with the club. When his glass of whiskey got low, he said to me, "I need a refill, little missy. Do you think you can get all of us back to the house in one piece?"

My sticky palms sweated in fear as I gripped the steering wheel and veered the cart across the perfectly manicured putting green, terrified that if we crashed, I'd again be a brat.

When I headed straight for a tree, he yanked the wheel so hard my sister flew off the back of the cart. He scolded her, "Now, you're all right. Get back on. This time hang on! With your poor handshake, it is no wonder you fell off. And let me tell you another thing—I don't like squealers. So, don't go crying to your mother that you fell off, waa waa. I don't like little crybabies."

Back at the house, he instructed me, "Grab some bottles of Coke for you brats, and don't forget my bottle of whiskey."

On our way back to the driving range, I accidently hit the brake pedal. My sister's mouth collided with the glass Coke bottle and chipped her front tooth!

Thirty-five years later, at the Animal Adoption Center, a family came in and the parents offered their young son and daughter's services to volunteer. Out of nowhere, I turned into my whiskey-soaked, loving uncle Russ.

I introduced myself by leaning over to the two young kids and informing them that we didn't provide free babysitting, and this was not a petting zoo. If I'd had a big fat cigar, I would have taken a long drag.

But, I said, they could stay if they liked animals and wanted to help them. Their parents stared at me but made no comments. Then I told them to look me in the eye and shake my hand. Both kids had sticky hands with soft grips that reminded me of overcooked pieces of pasta.

I leaned over and barked in their small, frightened faces, "Is that all you got, kid? I need to know you can hold a broom and work. You can pet the animals later. First, we need to make sure they've been well cared for. You like your food, water, and a warm bed. I bet you like to feel fresh and clean. Well, my little friends, these are only a few of the things we do for our cats and dogs here at the Center." I shoved my hand in front of them and again told them to look me in the eye. "Now show me what you got, kid, and make it count. Don't worry; I can take it."

I don't smoke cigars, drink whiskey during the day, or hang out at private driving ranges. Most days, my hair is ungreased, unless I'm too busy to shower. However, my voice does sound like I ate bowl of broken glass for breakfast. Thanks to my uncle Russ, I have one heck of a handshake and will look directly into someone's eyes and fake it, even if I am afraid.

During the Animal Adoption Center's first four years, there were hundreds of kids who came to pet the animals. When I was busy, sometimes they got away with it.

The kids who showed up at the adoption center came from a variety of backgrounds. Some were from the ten-thousand-square-foot estates spread throughout our valley. These upper-crust brats were dropped off by their nannies who arrived in new Teslas, BMWs, or Mercedes.

Then there were the concerned, caring middle-class parents who knew that, for their children, volunteering was the right thing to do. These parents drove Subarus, Volvos for extra safety, or Toyota Priuses to save the environment.

Kids whose parents suffered from hopeless depression or addiction to alcohol or drugs, and hence had little to no presence of a parent, found their own way to the Center, too. Some of them were dropped off reeking of cigarette smoke, in wrinkled, dirty clothes, with unbrushed hair and teeth. Like our animals, they too were orphans. We quietly tucked them under our wings with extra loving care. Those were the kids who became our kids. We secretly adopted them and openly encouraged them with great affection and praise.

The rich kids didn't know that I'd ask their parents to support us with tax-deductible donations. The middle-class parents carefully monitored their children's progress and praised them for their good deeds. Since they sometimes hovered in the office, I'd often ask them to run errands for the Center.

I also visited the homes of our orphaned volunteers for an unofficial inspection to assess their situations. I'd check to see if there was food in the refrigerator, and if not, it would magically appear. I'd ask permission for their kids to sleep over at my house, and then take them out for meals. I'd give the kids and their parents my phone number and tell them to call me if they needed anything.

Our donors not only gave generously to our animals, but also to our kids who needed eye exams, prescription glasses, winter boots, warm jackets, or their first trips to the dentist. When the parents went on drinking binges or just couldn't get out of bed, their kids stayed with me or Linda. If we'd called social services, those kids would have been transferred to another town for foster care, which also would have involved changing schools and losing friends. Jackson did not have one single state-certified foster parent for children. I always let the sheriff know they were with us just in case anyone was looking for them.

There was one night when a shy twelve-year-old girl stayed late with me in the office. I asked, "Honey, where's your mother? She must be worried about you."

Her answer floored me. "Oh, she's probably in a bar playing pool with some guy. She's not worried about me. I can take care of myself."

I tried not to act shocked and asked, "What about dinner?"

"We might have some cereal at home, but I know the milk was bad this morning." She ended up spending the summer at the Center and slept at my house most nights until her mother left town with her.

Weak, soggy-handed, little animal-crazed brats grew into responsible, capable, fun-loving leaders. Free, skilled labor builds a sturdy foundation for a new nonprofit and is called volunteering. My friends teased me when they told me I was probably breaking all the child labor laws by allowing them to spend so much time working there.

Our kids did more than just help with our cats and dogs; they had genuine concern for them and took full responsibility for their care and, many times, their adoption. They'd beg their parents to take our dogs home and foster them overnight. It was no surprise they'd then cry and plead to adopt them, and most of them did.

The staff and I asked all of the kids who came to volunteer, "Are you going to help those who need you? Or are you going to look away? Your choice will decide the kind of person you will become and as well as the life you will live."

I think that kids are no different than adults. They need encouragement to set their goals and reach them. We all need to have accomplishments, which help us gain self-confidence. Young or old, rich or poor, everyone does better when they have a purpose, a reason to wake up in the morning, or when we share a common mission and belong to a group. Most importantly, children thrive when they're included in a loving family that focuses on teaching them to act responsibly, respectfully, and to be considerate of others. These were important things I learned later as a grown-up. When you invite someone to volunteer, you give them a gift. It is a gift that may change their life. It takes just one person to set goals, make the work fun, to oversee tasks and check that they are done well, and to appreciate each volunteer's contribution.

All new volunteer children started out by studying the animals on our website. Then they were given a copy of the presentation we delivered during tours of the facility. They'd study this at home in preparation for reciting it, along with descriptions of all the animals, to me or another staff member as an informal test.

Many times, we had to bite our lips to hold back grins and laughter when they gave their tour presentations and described the Center's animals. Their innocence was incredibly refreshing, and the kids taking their first real job seriously was commendable. Our kids gave most of the tours of the Center, and were rarely interrupted, except for questions. Many were complimented on their knowledge. We kept a large poster-sized sign on the wall with the national statistics of the intake of animals and euthanasia in shelters for them to refer to if they lost their place.

After they completed the verbal tour test to me or my staff, we shook their hands and hugged them. I usually tossed them on the couch and sat on them, screaming, "Let the fun begin, you little brat! You have joined the ranks and are now on our team! Wahoo!"

Our morning routine focused on ways to have fun and interact positively with our cats and dogs. We fed and watered the animals, tidied the cat room, walked the dogs, trained the dogs, and brushed the cats. We also played music and danced like we were on the *Ellen* show while we cleaned. I liked to sing into the mop handle and act like Cher. Our kids packed the overnight bags for the dogs that slept in foster homes every night. Together, we neatly made beds for the cats and dogs with clean blankets and pillows. There was an enormous amount of craziness, affection, and silly, goofy laughter with our kids. It was incredibly meaningful for them to take charge helping our homeless animals. We praised them for their efforts and for being responsible, thoughtful, caring young people. We told them they would go far in their lives with their kind, loving, and giving hearts.

Once a kid had proved themselves as a responsible volunteer, they were awarded a personal name tag. As an unofficial, unpaid member of the staff, they proudly wore our badge of honor.

Pandemonium ensued when our young volunteers brought their friends to become volunteers. One day, more than twenty new kids sat in the back office as they filled out volunteer forms. Our seasoned rock stars Amanda and Krystal showed them how it was done, and then they took them under their wings and trained them, occasionally getting a bit cocky, as if they owned the joint. There were many days when we had too many kids show up to volunteer, but they were put on a schedule to reappear later.

Our young, highly trained volunteers cared for our animals before we opened and tended to the cats in Kitty City on the weekends. They also helped adults fill out adoption and foster forms and secretly screened them for us. An eleven-year-old girl once whispered to me, "I'm not sure if they're qualified since they don't have a fenced-in yard, they rent, and they didn't put down the landlord's phone number."

I whispered back, "Thanks for the heads-up. Way to go. You're my kind of kid."

They manned our phones, answered questions, made ID tags for the dogs, and wrote thank-you notes to adopters, foster parents, donors, and fellow volunteers. While my cell phone was stuck to my ear, they happily pumped gas into the van and paid for it with my credit card. Amanda and Krystal knew how to spell my name and sign it in my handwriting. It was not forgery since they had my permission.

One morning, about ten of our kids were spread out on the floor in the back office. I peeked through the cracked door to see cats lying on their backs and dogs sleeping under their arms as they pasted collages of animal photos together. I'd come in the front, so no one knew I was there. I heard a ten-year-old boy say to a new group of kids, "When Cupcake calls you a brat, it's because she likes you. She calls it a 'turn of what a deer meant.'"

Our new, efficient office manager Martha laughed and kindly corrected him, "It's actually pronounced 'term of endearment'. It does mean she likes you."

Adoptions were celebrated with hugs, screams, high fives, and tears of happiness as I tossed the kids on the couch. They were asked to ring the old metal bell that hung on our wall. Kids took photos of the animals with their new families and posted them on our web page. Big adoption days sent us on ice cream runs with dogs sitting on the kids' laps. Like Uncle Russ, I carefully veered our old, donated van from side to side in the empty back parking lot. This gave me a chance to remind the kids not to tell their parents and that "I hate squealers! Now hang on, you brats, we're going on two wheels!" Tapping the brakes left gobs of ice cream on their faces and they giggled when the dogs took big chomps out of their cones.

I'm not a big fan of children—or many adults. So many people tend to be self-absorbed, selfish, and addicted to their stupid cell phones (Okay, I am included in that criticism). I still agree with Uncle Russ, though—all kids are brats until proven otherwise.

What I despise most is a lazy, spoiled kid or adult who whines and doesn't know how to work. Our kids were not allowed to whine. If they made that mistake and complained in front of me, I'd ask if them if they needed to go home.

Our homeless cats and dogs didn't whine. Why should the kids complain when they were free to leave? My sixty- to seventy-hour workweeks gave me permission to occasionally feel sorry for myself, and my staff had full authority to tell me to knock it off if I went on too long and started to become a whiny martyr. Like I said, no one likes a whiner. Some of the kids may have started out as whiners, but we shut that show down. They were taught to keep trying and became winners while having a good time. Just because things don't always work out the way you have planned, it doesn't mean you have lost.

After four years working in the shared building with the boutique, I began to search for a new location for the Center. I'd been looking for several months when one night, as I lay awake in a state of fear, it hit me like a brick! Our kids could find our new location; they had the time, enjoyed a challenge, and lived on the internet. Why was I wasting my time?

For my bait, I put one hundred, one-dollar bills of my own money into a glass jar on my desk, and taped a note to it that read: "You brats find our new location to win!" That's my way of delegating. Early the next morning, it was Amanda and Krystal who sat on the back step of the Center. They were waiting for me with huge smiles, and interrupted each other as they yelled, "I found five places for us to look at!" Twelve hours after the bait had been set, they'd found our new location. The delegation, or the trap, had worked, and we signed the lease later that day.

After we toured our new building, we returned to our office and I tossed all the dollar bills in the air in the back office and screamed, "Wheeeeee! Way to go! You are my two top brats!" That night, the girls ate pizza with wads of dollar bills jammed in their jean pockets and red marinara smeared on their faces. They lay on big dog beds in the back office and bragged to each other with their mouths full. The Center could not have stayed open without them. They'd soon take over my job. I dubbed them my Junior Executive Directors.

They will never know how vital they were to our success or the never-ending joy and sheer happiness they brought into our lives. Our animals needed them. I hated being in the office without them. My outstanding, precious, hardworking, loveable brats often saved the day. Kids with mushy handshakes could have been lazy and watched TV or texted all day. Instead, our staff mentored them, and they became the backbone of our organization, entrusted keepers of our orphans who educated our visitors. All our lives were deeply enriched when we worked together as a loving family.

Osborne and little Baby Charlotte

Sneaking into
the Osbornes'

I received a call from a cat-rescue lady in Idaho. We'd never met, but she'd heard about me and the AAC, and begged me to take a pregnant cat. Having an extra bedroom that wasn't being used, I said, "Sure," and then asked her when the kittens were due.

She answered, "Oh, in a week, maybe two."

We met the next day in a megastore parking lot in Idaho. The woman was chubby with large, thick-lensed glasses, and she wore a pink sweatshirt with kittens on the front. She seemed to be in a hurry when she jumped out of her car and shoved the crate into my back-seat. Smiling, she handed me the cat's medical records. Before I had a chance to ask her any questions, she turned and walked quickly back to her car, waved, and sped off. Her rushed behavior felt odd to me. Something was not right.

In the crate was a young, stunning, black-and-gray striped cat with emerald-green eyes. The poor mama looked like she'd swallowed a watermelon. This lovely cat should have a beautiful name, I thought, and asked her, "How about Charlotte? It rhymes with harlot, and you must have been promiscuous, given your current condition, my dear."

I was headed to the grocery store to grab a few things when she suddenly let out a bloodcurdling scream. Frightened she was hurt, I pulled over to see if she was all right. Inside the crate lay a wet, teeny-weeny striped kitten. Charlotte carefully cleaned her baby, which was the spitting image of her. LBC, Little Baby Charlotte, was the firstborn.

I smiled but felt sorry for Charlotte. "A week? Really? How about five stinking minutes? Oh well, you'll feel better soon, Mama."

I moved the crate to the front seat, covered it with a blanket to give the young mother some privacy, turned up the heat, put on soft music, and took an occasional peek inside. There was nothing I could do now but drive back to Wyoming. Within an hour, Charlotte gave birth to five itty-bitty, three-inch-long, pink-nosed babies. I swear she had such a look of relief on her face after the last kitten was born. I'm not trained as a vet tech or a kitten midwife, but fortunately, Charlotte instinctively knew what to do. All five kittens were alive and bleating tiny, shrill mews as she meticulously groomed them.

Charlotte bringing those kittens into the world in the front seat of my car was a first—for both of us. She should have been spayed, and never should have had kittens. But she did, and her babies were lucky to have been born in my car and not outside in a field, or in a high-kill shelter.

Her kittens ultimately found loving families and had everything they needed. They were the fortunate ones. At the time of their birth, I didn't know how fortunate we would be as well: one crabby man's life was changed because of those little black-and-white darlings.

After I arrived home from picking up Charlotte, she and her little brood spent a single night at my house before another call came in for me to take two dogs. Charlotte's nursery was needed, or the dogs would be euthanized. It was time to call MBF Linda.

Linda and her husband, Oz, had recently purchased a large house to fix and flip. On their second floor, they had empty bathrooms and bedrooms. I'm not ashamed to admit that I had taken note of that empty space, and how perfect it would be for foster animals. I said to Linda, "Well, I can bring over a couple of wild, untrained young dogs or a litter of one-day-old kittens with their mother. You choose."

Linda laughed, "Either way, Oz is going to kill you. But then again, he's always mad at you, so really, what's the difference?" For years I'd been dropping off shelter animals for Linda to foster, and although

Oz and I had gotten along famously before my obsession started, now he seemed to have lost his love for me. Many times, he cringed and stomped out of the room when I showed up. He knew there was a cat or a dog in my car that needed to stay at their home. We never asked for his approval, as we knew he would say no. We knew it was safer to ask for his forgiveness than try to get his permission. Once he laid eyes on the cat or dog, he never denied them a temporary home under his roof. But he did complain and sometimes even whined.

I believe his first real animosity toward me started when Bailey the beagle stayed in their garage for a few nights. There was no music playing, but for some reason that dog danced on the hood of Oz's car all night long. Then there was the toothless schnauzer who had an accident on their carpet. Oz didn't see it until he stepped on it—barefoot, of course. Don't misunderstand me—Oz is a wonderful person, a genuine cat and dog lover. He just didn't sign up for all the animals that were constantly being dropped off. His home was not as neat and tidy as it was before I came into his life.

I replied to Linda, "Good point. Do you think we could sneak the kittens into the upstairs bathroom while he's at work?"

"Yeah, they will be easier to hide than a couple of dogs—it might work. You know he'll find out and curse your name, but he'll get over it eventually. We've never had a litter of kittens before. He might actually like that, since he loves cats so much."

The ruse didn't last long. The next morning, Oz ran upstairs to grab something out of the spare bedroom closet, and their housecat Stanley followed him. When Stanley hissed and growled, sensing intruders behind the bathroom door, Oz discovered Charlotte and her babies tucked away in the bathroom. Given his response, I am certain he would have slapped a restraining order on me if it had been those rowdy dogs hiding in the bathroom!

The next time I saw Oz, he was in Charlotte's bedroom sitting on the floor, mauling the adorable fluffy kittens and their mother. I waited for my scolding. He was smiling and didn't act crabby or make any snide remarks to me.

He said, "You know my face hurts from smiling so much since these damn kittens showed up. Oh, and just so you know, Charlotte is a perfect mother." And then *his* blabber attack began. In Oz's expert opinion, she was way too thin to be nursing, so he'd gotten special food from the vet to feed her so she could produce enough milk for her babies. He went on to say that Charlotte's kittens were not average kittens. Apparently, they were extremely intelligent, and each one had an exceptional personality. I mused, When had Oz become such an expert on kittens, or a nursing coach for a cat? He was a precious foster father—a kind man who took caring for his litter of damn kittens and their gorgeous mother seriously.

He continued, "Sometimes Charlotte looks tired and needs me to help, so I wash the babies with a warm washcloth."

I thought, Who is this guy? This was someone I'd never met before and not the usual crabby husband who scowled and slammed the door when I stopped by.

Oz explained to me that the bathroom floor was heated and that it kept Charlotte's kittens warm and cozy in their bed. He'd put up a baby gate with a chair inside the open bathroom door as an escape route for Charlotte when she needed a break. I marveled at clever Mr. Crabby Pants making such a great setup for those damn kittens and their gorgeous but thin mother.

Linda told me that as soon as he woke up each morning, he'd go straight to the kitchen, grab Charlotte's food, and run up to her bedroom where he would feed her his specially-made concoction to keep her weight up while nursing.

One day, Linda and I were together at my house when her phone rang. After answering, she whispered to me, "Oh boy, it's Oz." Although he was not on speaker, he was talking loudly enough for me to hear. He sounded desperate. "Linda, where are you? Charlotte is out of her canned food. Please stop at the vet on your way home, and hurry. They close in an hour!"

Linda hung up and said, "In the twenty years we've been married, I have never seen him act like this. Oz would have been a great dad."

Smiling, she continued, "I walked up to Charlotte's bedroom yesterday, and Oz was on the floor with the kittens. He didn't hear me, but I heard him talking to the babies, saying, 'Now this is not your permanent home, so don't get too comfortable. Your aunt Cupper pulled another fast one on us. One of you might be able to stay. Maybe you, LBC. We will have to see, but I love all of you the same.'"

It was Kitten TV, twenty-four hours a day, seven days a week at the Osborne home. Once the babies grew big enough to be outside, Oz propped a canoe against the side of the house for them to safely play under, out of sight of possible predators. Like a mother hen, he constantly counted them to make sure that everyone was in sight as he raked the lawn and weeded the garden.

The kittens ran out from under the canoe and did somersaults, ran sideways, pounced on grasshoppers, and chased butterflies. When it started to get dark, Oz carefully placed each one into a wicker basket, brought them inside, and put them into the suite he had designed just for them. The kittens were irresistible, and Oz was in heaven. Had it not been for the sneak attack I pulled, it's possible we never would have seen this side of him.

His babies grew up faster than we wanted, and Charlotte filled out nicely with sleek, shiny fur. Unfortunately, Linda and Oz were unable to keep any of the kittens. Their cat Stanley was furious that those damn kittens and their mother had invaded his home. He hated Kitten TV and wanted the channel changed. Linda and Oz reluctantly honored his wishes. The kittens were adopted into caring homes after being spayed, neutered, and vaccinated. A neighboring family who had regularly visited the kittens, and who had become enchanted with Charlotte, adopted her and made her part of their family.

As for you, Oz, I know where your key is hidden. Don't think I won't do it again.

Mr. Teeples

Mr. Teeples and Oz

Shortly after Oz was transformed by Charlotte and her brood's arrival, I received yet another call from a shelter that asked me to take a few dogs. Linda asked Oz if he'd drive over to get them. Oh, he would do it—anything for a reason to drive his vintage Porsche. He said sure, but only if he could drop them off at my house for the night. Linda warned him not to pick up any cats from the shelter, because their cat room had cats with distemper. But Oz is a cat man and quite fond of the dark stripers.

Linda called me later and said, "Well, Oz is back with the dogs. He listens to instructions about as well as you do. He picked up a cat when he was there. Parker asked him to take a big tomcat he'd found wandering around on Teeples Street."

He was Oz's favorite kind of cat: a big, gorgeous male tabby, a dark striper. Linda said, "It looks like he's had a bad injury: one eye is covered with scar tissue, so he's probably blind in that eye." She giggled, "Oh, and Cupper, you're going to love this. He's also cross-eyed."

We both laughed, and I said, "I can see why Oz had to take him; he sounds like our kind of cat." Parker had named him Mr. Teeples.

Oz knew his cat Stanley did not want to share his home with another cat, so he promised to keep Mr. Teeples quarantined in their garage. I started to complain, and Linda cut me off, saying, "Lighten up and back off. He can rescue one cat after everything we put him through. Oz is in love with the big fathead. He's in the garage talking to him right now while he's working on his bicycle. They're watching the Tour de France together."

She was right; no harm had been done, so long as Mr. Teeples stayed at their house in quarantine. Now Oz had someone to watch the race with, someone he could spoil. Mr. Teeples's life had been saved, thanks to Oz and Parker. Mr. Teeples was given a bicycle repair class in Oz's garage, which was covered in Lance Armstrong posters (pre-doping scandal, pre-dating Sheryl Crow. Like I said, we all make mistakes).

Once Mr. Teeples had finished his time in quarantine, it was time to get him neutered. When I arrived to bring him to his appointment, Oz had a strange look on his face. "I have some bad news. Teeples ran past me and got out of the garage this morning; I couldn't catch him."

"So, you lost an unneutered cat?" I asked. As if that weren't bad enough, I'd have to cancel the vet at the last minute on a Monday morning.

I told Oz that Mr. Teeples probably ran off because he'd made him watch the taped Tour de France over and over. To the best of my knowledge, most cats also have absolutely no interest in tuning up bikes! Cats like to watch fishing shows or a *National Geographic Wild* special on rodents. Irritated for a few minutes, I reminded myself that things like this happen with animals; it was no one's fault. God knows I have made plenty of stupid mistakes.

We went door to door and asked the neighbors to call us if there was any trace of our dark-striped, cross-eyed, fatheaded, unneutered friend. Out here in Wyoming, coyotes, foxes, and birds of prey live in our backyards. Cats that spend nights outside normally don't come home. A month later, we'd lost all hope that Mr. Teeples was alive. Indoor cats live an average of twelve years, while outside cats generally live for only two.

About a month later, Linda and I were shopping when we ran into Patti, Linda's neighbor. She practically ran across the store to talk to us. "Hey, you two! How is the world of animal rescue? Wait till you hear what happened to me and Hal a few weeks ago. Hal and I got home from a movie and found this big cat asleep in our bed. He must have come in through our old dog door. Hal thought I had slipped him in behind his back because I've been begging him to get a cat. But he's not really a cat person and doesn't like them. The strange thing is, he is now absolutely nuts over this cat. He is super friendly and interested in everything we do, following us around all day long. After the first night Hal said, 'Patti, we should keep him!' This guy acts as if he's lived with us all his life! Can you believe that I wished for a cat and then one just came straight into my house?"

When she finally stopped talking, Linda asked, "Does he have a big scar on one eye?"

Patti said, "Oh my God, yes! How did you know?"

I said in a British accent, "By any chance, is he slightly cross-eyed?"

Patti squealed, "Oh my gosh, he is cross-eyed!"

We burst into laughter. I continued in my fake British accent, "My dear Watson, it appears as though the mysterious disappearance of Mr. Teeples has finally been solved. Patti has busted this case wide open!"

Patti told us that Hal had named him Carlos. She continued, "When Hal's at his desk, Carlos sits in an open drawer; and in the kitchen, he sits on his stool next to the stove while Hal cooks. He sticks his head around the shower curtain to check on Hal while he's in the shower. It is kind of funny the way Carlos has attached himself to Hal and completely reformed him."

Patti's wish for a cat had come true. Like the exceptional cat that he was, Mr. Teeples got himself adopted, saved us money at the vet, and converted Hal into a crazy cat lover. We were ecstatic to know that Mr. Teeples had not only survived but was thriving in his chosen new kingdom. The fatheaded, cross-eyed king reigned over his chosen domain, just a few houses from Oz and Linda's.

Daisy

Johnny Lawless
and Daisy

Johnny Lawless wore an old-fashioned mustache, beat-up boots, and a dusty cowboy hat. I bet, given the chance, Johnny would have run with the likes of Butch Cassidy and the Sundance Kid. You could say he was a vigilante, protecting the helpless and personally ensuring that justice was served. The logo for his landscaping business was a shotgun barrel crossed with a shovel. At six-foot-three, he was not only tall, but also extraordinarily strong, with big shoulders and light-blue eyes against his handsome browned face.

True to his Irish nature, Johnny dearly loved his sweet mother Clare, his brother Anthony, and his best friend Virgil, a little, short-haired, gray-and-white striped cat with a little gray mustache under his lip that gave him a villainous look. With a grin on his face and a glint in his eyes, Johnny spoke of them quite often.

After a long day at work, Johnny would find Virgil to play what he simply called "the game." They would tear through the house, stalking and chasing each other as things flew off counters and dishes crashed to the floor. Virgil was quite sly and knew the game well. He would hide, ambush Johnny, and sink his sharp little cat teeth into his leg. This would only encourage Johnny to scream, "Oh, now you better hide and run now, little man. Game is on! I am going to get you!"

I first met Johnny because some mutual friends wanted to fix us up. My relationship with Olaf had ended, but my broken heart still ached and left me uninterested in dating. Johnny had just broken it off with his longtime girlfriend. One of our mutual friends said, "Now, if you two were in the same room, someone just might get hurt!" My curiosity set in, and I agreed to meet him. Lawless had a reputation for many things, like his crazy sense of humor, powerful sense of justice, and loud, uncontrolled laughter.

Johnny is one hardworking man who owns big trucks and runs backhoes and chainsaws for his landscaping business. He uses enormous tree spades to dig out huge trees from the forest to plant on his jobs. It was on the first snowy day in late fall that we met. We drove the Idaho countryside in his new red one-ton truck hunting trees for him to dig. Was this a vigilante lumberjack's idea of a first date? I went along for the ride to get to know him. The serene, wide-open fields of farmland had been harvested, and they slept dormant under enormous patches of drifted snow.

We drove silently and admired the miles of open farmland. We had gone about thirty minutes into our hunt when Johnny looked over to the right and suddenly stomped both feet on the brake pedal. We slid around on the thick layer of ice and stopped perfectly in the opposite direction on the road.

He laughed, and in a goofy voice said, "I love doing that. I feel like I'm on *The Dukes of Hazzard.*"

Shaken a bit, I nervously asked, "Hey Bo, where are we going?" (Bo Duke was one of the lead characters of the show. Yes, I am so old that I watched it as a kid.)

He said, "Let me tell you, I'm not happy. There is something I need to take care of right now. Hang on a minute and you'll see for yourself."

He pulled into a long driveway that led up to a huge metal barn, and slammed the truck into park. He looked to his left at a pile of snow, and his jaw tightened. He opened the door, got out, and slammed it shut. That's when the pile of snow exploded. What appeared to be a pile of snow was a black, frozen goat, its fur covered in ice. The goat shook its head from side to side so hard that it fell, spread-eagled, on the ground. That's when Johnny's fists clenched.

The goat's long legs looked like pool cues, and her ears reminded me of black banana peels attached to her head. Her golden eyes shone distinctly against her ice-covered face.

Johnny picked her up, brushed the ice off her long eyelashes, and, as he whipped open the door, he planted a quick kiss between her eyes and placed her behind me in the cab of his shiny new truck. He pulled out a few granola bars from the center console, ripped them open, and fed them to her.

He said abruptly, "Let's go. I have had enough of this." I quietly followed behind him as he marched toward the double-wide trailer. He said, "Let me do all the talking. No matter what, she is coming with us." His big hand punched the metal door and left a small dent. My eyes widened and I thought, Oh boy, someone is in deep trouble, and I'm glad it's not me.

This was getting interesting. He was no ordinary guy, and there was a frozen black goat in his brand-new truck to prove it. A small, pale-faced man in striped overalls answered the door. His face was expressionless. Stranger than his helpless appearance were the seven children behind him who stood silently around their mother, in a rocking chair nursing a tiny baby.

I stood behind Johnny as his deep, loud voice bellowed, "Allow me to introduce myself. My name is Johnny Lawless. I drove by your place last month and noticed the way you've been treating your little goat. She's got no shelter from the wind and was covered in snow, and now her ears are frozen! If that's not bad enough, there's no food or water out there. How would you like to be tied up outside like that? It looks like you feed your kids and your wife—why not your goat? Now you tell me, what do you have to say for yourself?"

The meek farmer barely uttered words loud enough for us to hear. He squeaked, "Well, now, the kids were going to practice roping with her, but they never got around to it."

Johnny exhaled loudly through his nostrils. "Now you listen to me. She is a living creature that feels pain, and she is in pain because of you. I won't have it. She is coming with us. Let me tell you something else: I'll be back to keep an eye on you. If I ever see you with another animal that you're not taking care of, I may not be so nice next time. When you call the sheriff, tell him Johnny Lawless paid you a visit. It's spelled just like it sounds!"

Back at the truck, I smelled the frozen goat's fur slowly thawing as she licked crumbs from the crevices of his new leather seats. When her rescuer jumped into the front seat, she playfully grabbed his hat, yanked it off, and let out a loud, "Maaaa!" Johnny laughed so hard he snorted. In an intentionally dumb tone of voice, he said, "Well, I've got a new tree spade, a new truck, a lot of payments, and no trees to sell. But we got her out of there, so it is a good day. Let's call her Daisy. I like that name—it reminds me of flowers and spring."

I wondered if it was for Daisy Duke on the show, Bo Duke's cousin.

He went on and on about this little, precious black goat who stood behind us in the cab of his brand-new truck. Her damp smell reminded me of the barns I'd played in as a kid and of my pet goat, Jacob, whom I had grown up with. He asked me what I thought she might like to eat and where she should sleep. Most importantly, he worried if Virgil would take to her.

When we stopped at the grocery store, Daisy and I stayed in the truck. People pointed and laughed at me with a goat riding shotgun inside the cab of a brand-new $60,000 truck. I didn't care what people thought. I just waved and smiled. Our Daisy adventure had given me greater happiness than any date I'd ever been on, if it was an actual date at all. Inside the grocery store, Johnny picked a small vegetable garden for her from the produce department. After he returned to us, he mixed a large salad in a bucket from the back of his truck.

Her golden eyes, with their long, soft, black lashes, stared into his eyes as she chewed, grinding her jaw sideways. She mumbled, "Maaaa maa," as vegetable pulp fell onto the floor of the truck. Maybe she was thanking him in her eating frenzy. She rode between us in the front seat, and the two of them looked adoringly at each other as we drove to the vet's office.

The pretty young veterinarian told us that goats are desert animals and cannot withstand cold, bitter winds. Johnny had been right— Daisy's little banana peel ears were frostbitten. The vet trimmed her overgrown hooves and handed us medicine along with instructions as to what food to buy at the feed store. Then the vet shyly glanced at Johnny and said, "No charge for today."

I thought, You can get in line, sister, and by that, I mean the back of the line; Daisy and I are in front of you. But it was clear that Daisy was the only one in his thoughts. That was alright with me. I was impressed by his guts to confront the people who neglected her.

For the next month, Daisy followed him around like a dog, and jumped sideways off everything she could climb. Johnny had planted a small forest of trees in his backyard for future landscaping jobs. She frolicked through his tree nursery, snapped off branches and ate the dead leaves while he pleaded with her to chase him.

Daisy didn't care about "the game," or maybe she didn't understand his need to be chased. His game of hide-and-seek would remain a sacred ritual between him and his beloved Virgil. Instead of chasing him, Daisy butted his behind with her head, and he squealed like a wild kid. I'm not sure who had more fun, but one thing is for sure: it wasn't Virgil. He watched this nonsense from the kitchen window with his ears flattened to his head. Johnny begged him to sit with Daisy in the heated garage during the day. Instead, Virgil hissed, spit in her eyes, and lashed at her face with his claws—a spoiled-rotten cat gone jealous. If Virgil could have made a voodoo doll of Daisy, he would have, and then stabbed a pin in and cursed her to run out of his life.

Daisy did fine if she had company, but when she was left alone, she bleated nonstop. She'd whip herself into a hysterical mess, as if she were an abandoned baby. She needed another four-legged friend to spend her life with.

I made a few phone calls and found a ranch in Wyoming where the winters were less harsh, and Daisy would be able to sleep safely in a warm barn with horses. She'd also have goat friends to play with during the day. When horses are injured, goats will often stay in their stalls as companions while they recover. Horses and mules in the pastures keep sheep, goats, and colts safe by kicking coyotes, wolves, and cougars with their hind legs when they try to attack.

The pouty landscaper made the four-hour drive to drop Daisy off with her new friends. After he returned, he said pitifully, "When she was turned out with her new friends in the pasture, she reared up and butted heads with her new buddies. She looked back at me, but only for a second. She was happier than I'd ever seen her."

I tried to console him, "Well, she is a goat. Animals don't get as emotionally attached to us as we do to them. They're wired to survive and don't mope around like humans, who have pity parties for themselves." Animals move on and live in the moment, while people are often challenged in that department and have many attachments.

Johnny turned his head and looked at Virgil's back, which was turned toward us. Virgil twitched his ears as he listened to our conversation. Johnny took notice, and put his finger to his lips, letting me know to stay quiet. He rolled a gum wrapper into a tiny ball and spit it through an empty ballpoint pen, nicking the tip of Virgil's ear.

"Hey, you little creep, you better be ready to catch up on the game." Virgil's gray ears flattened tightly against his head when he dove behind the couch. When Johnny walked past the couch, Virgil pounced, and with all four legs wrapped around Johnny's shin, he sank his sharp teeth into his kneecap. Johnny screamed, "Now that really hurt!" Maybe this was Virgil's payback for allowing Daisy to steal Johnny away.

Johnny tripped and fell to the floor with a loud thud. His eyes widened as he pulled himself to his knees. He shouted, "Oh, yeah! Game on, little man!" Once again, house plants, coffee cups, and whatever else got in their way, smashed to the floor. Life went back to normal for the handsome Irish vigilante landscaper and his sly, spoiled, ninja cat, Virgil.

We had a great time that day we hunted for trees and, of course, got Daisy from the farmer. A few times we laughed so hard we could not breathe. Soon after, Johnny got back together with his girlfriend, and I stayed happily single. To this day, he has not seen another animal where Daisy was once tied.

Finding Foxy

Foxy

Thanksgiving Day is not a day I look forward to. My coworkers have families, so I normally work to give them the day off. My family is far away, and I have no children or husband of my own. However, there was one Thanksgiving that stands out in my mind. MBF Linda and I told the AAC staff to take the day off and made plans to clean Kitty City with help from two of our volunteers, nine-year-old Krystal, and ten-year-old Amanda. Linda and I had personally but unofficially adopted these girls as our own, and as we drove through town that cold morning to pick them up, we noticed something odd: there were no other people or cars on any of the city streets. We wondered if everyone had traveled out of town to see relatives.

We were just a few blocks away from Amanda's house when Linda pointed toward a side street, "Stop! Cupper, did you see that?" There was urgency in her voice. "Turn around; go back. There's something strange in the road."

I flipped a quick U-turn, and we watched as a small animal wobbled in the road and then slowly bumped into the curb. The strange little creature stumbled and fell; my heart hurt as we watched it struggle to get back up.

I turned down the side street, and Linda got out and cautiously picked up the tiny, matted little dog. She slowly slid back into the passenger seat and placed it on her lap. She gasped, "Oh my God, the poor thing is emaciated. Oh no, her left eye is missing." Then she winced, "You're not going to believe this; they're both gone. She's completely blind."

I screeched, "What! Are you kidding me?"

She sobbed, "Oh no, Cupcake, I am not kidding." We silently stared at two deep, empty sockets on the dog's face. Linda whispered, "How could anyone starve a little helpless dog and let her wander around blind on the streets alone? It's freezing out there, and she's going to get hit by a car."

We had been in dozens of animal shelters, rescued hundreds of animals, and seen unspeakable things I don't care to recall. But we'd never seen a dog without eyes. The scrawny dog relaxed as Linda's tears landed on her back. "Feel her spine . . . She is a rack of bones."

All she had was a thin layer of dry, dirty fur that covered her back. I pulled my jacket off, and together we wrapped her up in it like a burrito. I shook my head several times, opened my eyes wide, and tried to reassure Linda that everything would be all right. But I was completely blown away.

I said, "Okay, now she's safe with us, not in the street frightened and alone. You know we were meant to find her. I am not calling the shelter. Whoever allowed her to get this thin and fall off the curb un-supervised can come looking for her. Good luck trying to get her away from me."

We stopped in front of Amanda's house and beeped the horn. The girls were excited at the sight of the new animal wrapped in my jacket. They asked, "What have you got? Where did you get that dog?"

Then they noticed we were upset and asked, "Are you crying? What's wrong?" They both inhaled loudly when Linda pulled off the coat and they saw the terrier's face. "Can she see? Does she have eyes? What's wrong with her?" We heard their muffled cries in the back as we explained how we'd found her walking on the road.

We pulled up to the adoption center and our two superstars jumped into action. You see, Krystal and Amanda were not ordinary kids. Although they were not even teenagers at the time, they were experienced in every facet of animal rescue and care. For the past few years, we had worked side by side with them and handled hundreds of animals together. Amanda gently pulled the little dog out of the jacket and then handed us some tissues, and hugged Linda and me. They said, "We have this one. We know what to do. She will be okay."

Amanda grabbed a clipboard with a medical record sheet and went to work "Well, it looks like we've a got a little girl here. Her nails have grown under and into her paws. I think she's a smooth-coated Jack Russell terrier. She must be hungry. Did you feel how skinny she is? Oh, my goodness, all of her teeth are really bad; her breath smells like rotten eggs."

Amanda gave our new friend a real dog jacket with a new little collar, while Krystal emptied a can of dog food into a bowl. I was still in a state of disbelief that we'd found a dog wandering the streets with no eyes, just empty sockets.

The only living thing we saw on the street that morning was this ratty-looking, starved-half-to-death Jack Russell terrier that was com-pletely blind. What were the chances that we, of all people, would be the ones to find her? This was no coincidence. Now we had a special guest for Thanksgiving and another reason to celebrate gratitude.

Jackson, Wyoming, is a place where millionaires and movie stars build large second homes in the mountains. Here, people spay and neuter their animals and adopt from shelters. Our community understood animal rescue and supported our nonprofit. They had adopted and fostered more than a thousand dogs and cats in our first three years of operation.

I wondered if someone from another county had dumped the dog in Jackson, hoping she would find a good home. No one from our town would commit such a heartless act.

I called the sheriff's office and told them if anyone called about this dog, they needed to call me directly. This little one was not going to the local shelter—she was staying with us.

The little terrier inhaled her dinner of canned food while the girls carefully trimmed what they could from her overgrown nails. We cleaned Kitty City as she lay in the center of the main room on an overstuffed bed in a new polar fleece jacket. Of course, the girls gave her a tiny blanket and shoved a few pillows under her to make her as comfy as possible. We laughed and made jokes while we planned our little one's Thanksgiving feast. Her pretty head turned back and forth toward each one of us as we spoke. She was alert, but her face was completely expressionless without eyes to read.

By this time in our rescue work, Linda and her husband Oz had grown apart. Eventually they both agreed they wanted different things in life, and it was time to live separately and end their marriage. It was an amicable break. Linda bought a darling, small log cabin, and I immediately claimed its back bedroom as my own. Her new home became my second home, and we were joined by dozens of foster animals. Linda's old log cabin was cozy and inviting without Oz there crabbing about all our rescue animals. That Thanksgiving, we dragged a full-sized mattress from Linda's spare bedroom into the living room. Using pillows, comforters, and blankets, we built a big nest for the Jack Russell in front of the old cast-iron fireplace. The little one was propped up in her new bed, and the girls took turns feeding her bits of chicken and small spoonfuls of mashed potatoes. We had a wonderful day laughing and debating over who was going to hold her and who was lucky enough to sleep with our newly found prized guest.

Several days after we had found our little one wandering the streets, a young man called my cell phone and said, "The sheriff's office gave me your number. You need to return my girlfriend's dog." My heart immediately sank. He went on to say that he and his young girlfriend had a baby. The baby had pulled on the dog's fur, and the dog had snapped at the baby. He also said that he preferred that the dog stay outside.

I said, "Have your girlfriend call me directly, and we will meet her in person."

I was wrong. Someone from our town did own this dog, someone who also had a new little human baby. Now we could find out why her eyes were gone. I snapped at Linda, "There's no way she's getting her back, no matter what she says. We will buy her if need be. She is not going back to a person who let her starve and wander the streets blind."

Linda said, "Hey, cool down, Cupper. Let me do the talking. I want to hear what she has to say for herself."

We walked into the hotel where the young mother worked at the front desk. She immediately asked if we knew how hard it was to raise a baby. I blurted, "Well, I hope you take better care of your baby than your dog." Linda stepped on my foot and glared at me to shut up. Baby or no baby, there were no excuses for neglecting her blind dog, as far as I was concerned. She could have reached out for help but had chosen not to.

The young woman said her mom bred Jack Russells, and she'd gotten the dog as a puppy from one of the litters and named it Foxy. Years after giving birth to Foxy, her mother had gotten glaucoma and went blind from the disease. Foxy was a young dog when she herself contracted glaucoma and had to have both eyes removed or they would have burst. The choice was to either remove them or put her down. And although having a child had displaced Foxy from her prime place, the young woman still loved her, and she cried tears of remorse and shame.

I showed the woman photos of Foxy's skeletal profile, and her hideous long-curled claws. Linda kindly explained that this was no way to treat any living creature. I stepped on Linda's foot under the table and said to the young mother that, if she signed Foxy over to us, we wouldn't press animal-cruelty charges against her. This was a bluff.

Her hand quivered slightly when she signed the paper that we had drawn up to transfer her ownership to us. Then she said, "I know you'll take better care of her than me. I never meant to hurt Foxy. She's . . . my baby. I mean, she *was* my baby."

I said, "Well, you did the right thing. She is our baby now. She will find a permanent home with tons of love, and she has received the medical care she needed."

That was it—Foxy was our dog. I ran out the hotel door into the parking lot and jumped up and down. Linda and I screamed and hugged each other as if we were star quarterbacks who had just won the Super Bowl. I kicked the envelope with Foxy's adoption papers and yelled, "Touchdown!" and pretended to dance like a chicken in the end zone.

Linda laughed and said, "Cupper, would you knock it off already?"

For Linda's birthday, I found a doormat that said, "This home is guarded by a Jack Russell terrier." I blackened out the eyes on the dog on the mat with a magic marker and added "with NFE (No Freaking Eyes)" to the tagline. Linda gushed like a proud mother the first time Foxy jumped onto the couch, shook a toy, and pulled out its stuffing. She restuffed the toy over and over, only for Foxy to shred it again. And Linda laughed every time as if it were the first time she'd seen her do it.

Foxy never felt sorry for herself like a human might have. She adjusted. Most of the time, she acted as if she had eyes and could see. We often had to convince people using my clinical explanation of NFE to make them fully comprehend that she was completely blind and had no eyes.

When it got warm, Foxy hung her head out the car window while she sat on Linda's lap. Once, at a stop sign, a squirrel ran in front of the car. Foxy smelled it, jumped out of the window, and chased it up a tree! Her front paws scratched at the trunk as she tried to climb, and she barked like a maniac. Linda had to pull her off the tree, wrestle her back into the car, and shut the windows. All the while, Foxy fought her like a pro-life protester resisting arrest.

We'd met a wonderful woman named Lisa through the AAC who was as insane about animals as we were. She worshipped terriers and generously supported our rescue. When she heard Foxy's story, she paid for her medical bills. Over the next few months, Lisa visited Foxy at Linda's house and secretly wanted to adopt her. It was during a Mother's Day brunch that Lisa finally got up the nerve to ask, "Is Foxy staying with you, or is she going to be adopted out? I mean, would you two consider letting me adopt Foxy?"

Linda didn't blink and replied, "I don't think so."

With the loving care from her doting, overly protective foster mother, she'd grown strong and confident, back into a true terrier. Foxy was ready, but her foster mother wasn't. I told Lisa we'd be honored to let Foxy be her baby. She would make a perfect home for Foxy, as she was experienced with the breed and had plenty of time for her. As she anxiously awaited Foxy's arrival, she shopped for new beds, toys, special food, and made additional vet appointments with specialists.

I didn't want to wrestle with Linda to get Foxy away, but I would have. We both knew our homes needed to stay open for new orphans. Our final gift to the animals we foster is to allow them to be adopted. Now when Thanksgiving comes, I fondly remember the special guest we were gifted to find and how much love a little skinny dog with NFE brought into all our lives. And that there are no coincidences in life.

The Big-Hearted Benefactor

I had sworn off dating and been single for several years. I had absolutely no interest in a new relationship. Olaf had been the love of my life, and my feelings for him remained deeply embedded in my aching heart. There was no other man for me. But. A man came into my life and played a vital role in our survival during the second year of operation at the AAC.

I believe we are all given strengths. I am blessed to have many, but business management is not one of them. After our first rocky year at the nonprofit, I conducted an informal investigation to find an experienced businessperson. In a small town, that means basically asking around to see if anyone could recommend such a person. One man's name came up several times: James. He was well-known throughout the valley as the best in his field as a top financial expert who had investigated and prosecuted federal fraud in the 1980s. Shortly after my search began, I ran into him at the bagel shop. I cornered him as he poured cream and five heaping tablespoons of white sugar into his coffee. After I introduced myself, I asked him if he would advise our nonprofit and join the board of directors at the Center. He put his hand up, laughed, and waved me back as he loudly slurped his sugary latte. He claimed that he was too busy going on vacations. He had retired and wanted to stay that way.

The next day when James walked into the Center, I was pleasantly surprised and thought maybe God or the universe had swayed him to accept my invitation to join the board. Instead, he asked me out to lunch. I accepted, knowing this was my chance to share more information about our organization.

After I opened the Center, I had no time for haircuts or bike rides. On most days, a shower was forfeited to clean my house before work, and a relationship, well, that was not a thought I entertained. I made it clear to him at lunch I was not interested in dating him or anyone, and that I had given up that part of my life. I shared my obligations with my volunteer kids, our foster parents, donors, and my dedicated staff. Our volunteer kids also worked hard, and our insane laughter and silliness got us through the ugly jobs we would have otherwise hated. With the cats, dogs, puppies, and kittens as the center of our lives, we were a big, happy family that knew how to get things done while having an absolute blast.

James ignored my refusals and persisted with lavish lunches and dinners at expensive restaurants, while I persisted and peppered him with questions and asked for his advice about the financial issues with the Center. I confess that his attention and being spoiled by him also made me feel special. We went to a Van Morrison concert in Colorado, and on a weekend shopping trip to San Francisco. It was his great love for shopping and beautiful things that quickly expanded my limited wardrobe. We ate like royalty and partied like we were rock stars on tour. We spent a lot of time together and laughed while covered in dogs.

What most people don't know is that he personally ensured our continued success when he wrote large donation checks that kept our doors open. That gave me peace of mind and the ability to sleep through the night. After a real night's sleep, I cried less during the day. He also generously opened his home to a nonstop junk show of animals from the kill shelter. We did get a financial person: while he was not much of an advisor, he was a secret benefactor. He was also an unbelievably loving and caring foster father. With him in my life, I had to juggle more things, but it was also suddenly filled with excitement. After he adopted me, I finally knew what it felt like to be well cared for and protected. My stomach no longer ached with the constant fear of failure or extreme hunger.

James commanded attention. He wore round, gold, antique glasses with blue lenses. He drove a boxy silver Mercedes that perfectly matched his thick, gorgeous hair that most men his age would have killed for. Most of the time, he wore a serious expression and used a deep, commanding voice, like a five-star general ready to enter battle at a second's notice. However, his battle would have been some sort of business deal. He enjoyed my crazy sense of humor and found it challenging. At times, he could act more ridiculous and be more sarcastic than me (which isn't easy). We were complete opposites: He loved material things, while I was a minimalist. He loved to eat; I preferred to starve and stay skinny. He was a well-known financial expert, and I hadn't balanced my checkbook in years.

My rental house at the time had served me well; it was hidden up a steep road on the side of the mountain pass in a dense forest of tall, old pine trees. I was humiliated by its rough condition. His frat house in college was probably nicer than my rental. My house was nothing more than a metal roof over a cinder-block foundation dug into the hillside. The few small windows kept it dim inside. Previously, it had been a repair shop for small engines.

Adding a kitchen sink, linoleum floor, and rough bathroom converted it into a money-making rental. To cover the cinder-block walls I absolutely despised, I sewed rich, pretty Ralph Lauren floral sheets into curtains and hung them on the walls. It was sad and lame but an affordable attempt to spruce up the former mechanic's shop. My flower gardens were beautiful, my windows were sparkling clean, and my antique furniture, including a fainting couch, made it livable for me and my foster animals.

My yard was like a wooded summer camp that you'd send your kids to, with a big fire pit in the center and a horseshoe pit down the hill. A friend had nicknamed my place "Camp Chickamunga." We all called it "The Camp." When dogs arrived to be fostered, my friends called it "Camp Cupcake for Dogs." Being the bunker that it was, it took many big hits with all the cats and dogs that made it their temporary home.

I pride myself on being a minimalist. The only things I value are my animals (surprise, surprise), along with my family, and my few, special supportive friends. For more than thirty years, I have managed the minutely detailed care for several of the huge estates in our valley, which belong to real-life royalty—a few billionaires, a worldwide movie star, and, of course, the mere millionaires. I have always been careful and conscientious of the owners' beloved, expensive objects in their mansions, which they refer to as "one of their vacation homes." My heart holds no jealousy for their wealth; my wealth cannot be measured by money. Believe me when I say I repeatedly warned the financial expert that I wasn't interested or available for a relationship. But in my limited free time, we had some seriously wild adventures. My life was full of daily trips to the vet, nonstop chaos, and my carpet cleaners were on speed dial. Yet, James persisted, day after day, until I finally conceded, accepted his generous invitation, and moved into his large, luxurious home, once featured in *Architectural Digest*.

I exercised extreme caution with my foster animals, but his house suffered a few significant hits after my arrival. It was not me who raised my voice; it was the silver-haired general. Of course, I understood and felt ashamed and repeatedly apologized. But with the nonstop parade of animals, a mess or damage to his home was inevitable. It was a lovely estate, after all, not a dog kennel. More than once, I grabbed my keys and dogs, quickly packed them into my old, donated dented van with faded, scratched paint, and ran back to my small, dark house where there were no housekeepers or large bronze sculptures on display.

I was grateful for my house. My kind, absentee landlords welcomed my rescue animals, and my place was affordable, private, quiet, and safe. Most importantly, my bunker at Camp Chickamunga could take big hits, given the concrete floor.

Inevitably, not long after fleeing his mansion and returning back to my home, I would find James at my front door, begging me to return. And I would, with dogs in tow, and eventually would bring more dogs from the shelter for us to foster. He was more than happy to be a good host to them. He sometimes begged the once-homeless dogs to lie on his expensive furniture. He relished his lounge time on his luxurious couches and thought the dogs would also share his deep appreciation for the finer things in life. It was a generous, loving offer on his part.

Unimpressed, they lifted their legs on the gorgeous furniture and barfed on the upholstery, all carefully chosen by his interior designer.

Later, I jokingly suggested that we cover the rare wood floors with a layer of sawdust. It may have made them easier to clean, although a wheelbarrow and a shovel leaning against the wall would have been a bit out of place next to James's exquisite art displayed in the private, professionally lit gallery that he called home.

His deep concern helped hundreds of animals that needed a home, along with giving them access to his bank account. He kept me healthy, took me to the doctor or dentist, and fed me in bed when I was too weak and sick to walk, or too hoarse to talk. He did the same for a dog whose leg had been amputated, or had an eye or teeth removed. He covered us with cashmere blankets on the couch and built massive fires that warmed us. The blue flames on the logs danced and often mesmerized me into a dreamy, safe, peaceful place. His sumptuous meals kept me from falling over when I tied my shoes after I'd skipped too many meals.

He often reminded me how proud he was of me for the animals we saved at the Center. "You have no idea how positively you have impact-ed so many people's lives when you find them their new best friends. I love all the dogs you bring home, and I can't believe they would have been put to death if you didn't take them. You do good work, Boo Boo." Our happiest moments were when his enormous, tastefully decorated living room was covered with more than a dozen dogs who slept on his furniture as we acted silly and drank wine in front the blazing fireplace.

Our precious Laney

Our Elaine

Frequently the AAC would adopt out all our animals, leaving us room to bring in more cats and dogs. On one of my rescue runs to the Idaho kill shelter, one of the workers walked with me through the dog kennels, indicating which dogs were available. Many of the dogs had just arrived and were required to stay for three days in case they had owners to reclaim them. After that, they were made available for adoption or euthanized to make room for the nonstop flow of incoming animals.

As we walked through the long rows of barking dogs, the shelter worker pointed and said, "Nope, that one's not ready to go yet," and "The owners are coming for that one." He finally pointed to a little, red collie mix and chuckled, "You can take this old thing. No one's gonna want her. We're gonna do her this afternoon when the vet comes."

I bent down and lifted her lip to see what condition her teeth were in and gagged at the smell of her ungodly breath. She placed her little, narrow paw on my leg. That's when I noticed the long patches of fur that stuck straight up between her toes. They reminded me of Grinch feet.

A dental and spay surgery would cost more than we had in the bank at the Center. The balances on my personal credit cards had been maxed out from vet bills since a year before I opened the Center. As I lifted her into the van, I looked into her cloudy eyes and kissed her bony face and told myself it would work out. I didn't care if I had to declare personal bankruptcy to save her—or any animal's—life. She was in the van on her way to a new life, not at the shelter waiting to be euthanized.

I was living with James at the time, and as we got closer to his magnificent home, I worried that he'd be upset that I was bringing home yet another dog. My duties as the executive director of the nonprofit had shifted over to mostly doing paperwork, putting out small fires, and delegating every job possible to the volunteers and staff. Gathering funding for the Center at that time also lay solely on my shoulders. However, I still took home many sick and injured animals with me every night, sometimes up to a dozen at a time.

In front of Mr. Fancy Pants James, I did my best to pretend to be a regular person. In truth, I am many things—but a regular person? Probably not a word anyone who knows me would use to describe me. A normal or, say, regular person does not have teeth marks in their checkbook, have their car door handles chewed off, occasional dog vomit in their purse, or have ten plastic dog crates neatly stacked in their living room. It was just a matter of time before James dumped me. No man in his right mind could tolerate the constant chaos of the three-ring-circus life I had chosen to live. My decision between a man and animals had been made long ago—I chose animals. We seemed to get along better.

I snuck the skinny, old, red collie into James's perfectly decorated home and into the guest wing bathroom for her first bubble bath. Just as I finished drying her off, James pushed the open door and gasped, "Rebecca, what are you doing in here? Oh my God in heaven, that is the most pathetic dog I've ever seen. She is emaciated! Daddy's going to heat up some chicken and rice right now for that poor, little old girl."

After she was towel dried, I wrapped her in a new thick blanket and carried her to the living room. James had started one of his raging fires. My mind drifted to thoughts of her hunger and neglect. I held back my tears for her misery, and for the animals I'd left behind at the shelter. James sat on the arm of the couch next to me and put his big warm hand on my back. "Babe, let's face it. There is no way we're letting anyone else adopt this skinny old girl. She's ours now." She had been in the house for less than twenty minutes when he said, "We're keeping her," and he then named her Elaine. Most of the time, we called her Laney for short. Just as I had suspected, everything did work out, and Elaine became our dog. Her new daddy was devoted to making her new life with us as perfect as possible.

Laney lost sixteen teeth at the vet's office and had her cancerous mammary tumors removed. James happily paid the enormous bill and treated her like a queen, serving her on his couch as she recovered. Her new daddy prepared soft, warm, delectable dishes for her three times a day. I melted every time he whispered in her ear that she was his pretty little baby. As we cared for Elaine, James and I became a family.

As for James, he did not dump me. As a matter of fact, he never said no to an animal in need. Instead, he helped me care for them and cooked special meals for those who had been starved. He paid the enormous vet bills that kept the Center's doors open. Hundreds of lives were saved thanks to his genuine concern and generosity.

Elaine slept between us in bed. James normally fell asleep with his hand wrapped around her neck and her head resting on his shoulder. Laney's favorite dinner was baked chicken from the deli, and her dedicated daddy tried to buy one for her every day. He fed chicken to all the dogs, but he always fed our Laney first. He referred to these feeding frenzies as "chickee-chick parties" for the dogs. He laughed like Steve Higgins, Jimmy Fallon's co-host on *The Tonight Show*, every time one of the dogs wolfed down a piece.

Thanks to James's amazing care of Laney, and to the outstanding care she received from her vet Dr. Katherine Luderer, not to mention the few hundred roast chickens, we were fortunate to have Elaine with us for almost two years. Laney lived out the rest of her life with great dignity as a cherished member of our family. Although her time with us was too short, we were extremely grateful for every day we had her in our lives. Loving our Laney led me to save more dogs like her, and her doting daddy made it possible.

King Arthur

King Arthur and the Squire

Linda and I were just getting ready to pull out of the parking lot at the shelter in Idaho when Parker, our good old boy, yelled as he walked towards us, "Hey, you gals forgot someone!" Our van was already packed full of crates with dogs on their way to new lives in Jackson at the AAC.

"Now come on, you gals have got to take him; he's going with you." Parker reached through the window of our van and carefully handed Linda a large, longhaired gray cat. Parker smiled, "He's kind of old and crippled up, but he is one hell of a cat! I promise you won't regret taking him. Every time I walk by his kennel, he reaches out and grabs me with both of his front paws."

I said, "Well, of course he does. He probably wants to know why he has been forced to live in a small metal cage for the past month. Thanks for running him out to us, Mr. Animal Control Officer of the Year!" We were packed full, so he sat on Linda's lap while I drove.

The gorgeous gray cat had a circle of bare skin around his neck where he'd once worn a collar. His back was bony, he'd been declawed on his front and back paws, and he had been neutered. By the size of his chubby little gut, we knew the cat had belonged to someone for a long time. I imagined his original owner had probably passed away or gone to live at a nursing home.

This distinguished older gentleman had a wise, handsome face with a condescending look, as if he were superior to everyone he met. On our way back to the AAC, we headed straight to our usual drive-through where we ordered burgers for the dogs and a fish sandwich for our new older feline friend. He inhaled his fish sandwich and growled as he chewed. Once he was finished, he yowled and pawed at the bag. When he demanded more, Linda said, "Now listen, your royal highness, one fish filet is all you get. I am sorry, but we are driving through two mountain passes to get home, and I don't want to wear your lunch."

I said to Linda that something about this cat reminded me of royalty. Linda then dubbed him King Arthur from Idaho.

Once we were back at the AAC, we placed Arthur safely in our cat room, Kitty City. That was when we saw Arthur pull himself across the floor. His arthritic back made it difficult for him to walk. My heart felt sick with worry. Arthur needed to come home with me, but James was terribly allergic to cats.

It was my birthday, which is just like any other day to me. James had made reservations at a wonderful, exclusive restaurant. It was a nice gesture on his part, but I would have rather stayed home with the dogs and Arthur. James had been nicknamed "Squire" in college for his smart clothing, impeccable manners, and old-world attitude. If there were such a thing as past lives, the Squire also must have been royalty (at least, in his mind he had been).

I refused to call James Squire. Instead, I dubbed him "Squie"! The other names I felt fit him best were Mr. Smarty Pants and Fancy Pants, but more often than anything, Mr. Bossy Pants. James wore beautiful clothing and handmade shoes from England. Dogs jumped on me, and cats snagged my clothes. I tried to dress well, but usually I had a lot of fur on my clothing or dirty paw prints on my pants. Some women love to wear diamonds or carry expensive purses. Not me. The only thing I loved wearing were my old beat-up, half-rotten cowboy boots and a dry-cleaned shirt.

We arrived late to the restaurant. We were seated in front of the fire at a special table James had requested. My clothes were nice enough but had a fair amount of dog and cat hair on them. My body was weak with fatigue, and my empty stomach gurgled from the acid that lingered from the morning's coffee. My mind was alert with an unsettled feeling when I thought about all the new animals we'd pulled from the shelter in Idaho. I tried to act interested in the conversation, but my head was preoccupied with Arthur and his limp back legs. We had a fabulous dinner, but when they served my birthday cake, I suddenly burst into uncontrollable tears of guilt and fear about Arthur.

James ushered the waiter away from the table and said, "What is it, babe?" I was unable to answer and sobbed like a baby. He said sternly, "You need a vacation. You've got to quit working all these crazy hours. How in the world do you think you're going to keep from having a nervous breakdown?"

A vacation would help, but right then I wanted and needed Arthur. The thought of him unsupervised in the cat room, alone without a person as I sat in this fancy restaurant, filled me with a hateful guilt. Once my tears let up enough to speak, I said, "We got a beautiful cat today at the shelter. He's older and disabled. You won't understand, but he's meant to be with me." A few years back, James thought it would be nice for his daughters to have a new pet and adopted a kitten for them. Shortly after the kitten arrived, he sneezed so uncontrollably that he fell backward and split his head open on a table. His extreme allergies had sent him to the hospital for stitches.

He stood up and quickly paid the dinner bill, and then savagely shoveled a few forks full of my untouched piece of cake into his mouth before we walked away from the table. Cake crumbs flew off his lips with his stern words, "You're going home and straight to bed, Boo Boo!" See what I mean about Mr. Bossy Pants? (I want to add that he normally had impeccable, almost snobbish, manners. I detest bad manners when eating.)

Back home, I collapsed into bed in my fur-ridden clothes, my face still streaked with tears. I couldn't stop crying. I cried for many reasons, most of which weren't clear to me. Let's just say the dam had broken. The next morning James woke me up and said, "Let's bring King Arthur home. I will take allergy shots, but he must stay in the spare bedroom."

Elated, I screamed, jumped out of bed, and ran to my van in the same clothes from the night before. When I entered Kitty City, Arthur was nowhere in sight. Frightened, I called out his name. A weak cry came from the corner of the room. It was Arthur. He hung listless, upside down, his back leg stuck in a chair. He was covered in urine and barely breathing, his heartbeat faint. My worst fear had come true. Now he was close to death, thanks to me leaving him in the cat room overnight. Our youngest and most-skilled volunteer, Krystal, walked into the cat room and found me sobbing as I rocked Arthur in my arms. She grabbed my shoulder and said, "Get a hold of yourself! You drive and I'll hold him. We have to go to the vet."

We went to my kind, wise vet Ken Griggs, who looked at old, injured Arthur and calmly said, "Well, we'll do what we can, but don't get your hopes up. We'll give this ole boy a chance. If he turns the corner by 4:00 p.m., you can pick him up. Otherwise, I'd say he's had enough, and we let the good old boy go to heaven."

I trusted Ken implicitly. Arthur's best chance of survival was with Ken and his trusted sidekick of twenty-five years, Carol. They had helped me save hundreds of animals before I opened the AAC. Carol walked us to the door and snapped, "Now quit your crying. That won't save him. He ain't dead yet! Go about your business, and we'll call ya later." Carol was strong; she had seen thousands of terrible accidents with animals. This was her way of consoling me. She was tough but wise like Ken, and she was also right: crying wouldn't change the outcome. All I could do was pray and hope that Arthur wouldn't suffer and die.

At 4:00 p.m., Ken laid our old gentleman down on the table and walked into another room to get the medicine that would end Arthur's life. He felt it was the right thing do, as Arthur had shown little to no improvement. Next to Arthur on the table, Ken left some ranch-flavored Pringles potato chips he'd been eating.

He returned to see that Arthur had pulled himself over to the pile of chips. He heard the loud crunching and said to Carol, "Well, looks like he may have turned the corner. I'll put a cast on his leg. Tell Cupcake to come and get him." Thus began our life with the little king.

Arthur and I arrived back at Squie's house to find a huge tuna sandwich with potato chips and a pickle on an antique china plate in the guest room. I laughed and said, "Come on Squie, you're over the top with the pickle."

Arthur was weak, but his appetite was incredibly strong. After he inhaled everything (minus the pickle), James affectionately tucked us into bed in the guest room. I insisted on sleeping with Arthur for fear he might die during the night. If he were to pass over to the other side, I wanted him to feel loved. Before we fell asleep, I thanked God that Arthur had lived and asked Arthur to forgive me. He slept soundly in my arms with his head tucked tightly under my chin.

The next morning, Squie came in and found us both well rested and Arthur hungry again. I didn't mind turning a year older, knowing Arthur could live with us. For breakfast, much to James's dismay, I reheated a piece of pizza. When I sat down next to Arthur, he used his paw to pull the pizza off my plate. Once again, he growled and chewed at the same time. I suspected this was probably not Arthur's first piece of pizza. He appeared to be quite skilled at stealing food, considering that he'd been declawed.

James had thoughtfully prepared a salmon omelet for his first breakfast, but Arthur turned up his nose and begged for more pizza. It was at that moment that Squie accepted his position as Arthur's minion and gladly reheated another piece of pizza for our little king. When Arthur was finished, he licked his paws and cleaned his face. Then Arthur licked my hand in appreciation for sharing my pizza with him. My happiness overwhelmed as he lay on my lap.

Arthur spent the warm afternoons perched on a big, red, velvet pillow, sunning himself on the porch at James's lovely house. He attentively attended our board meetings at the adoption center, tucked into a plush-lined wicker basket. He became a favored guest at many dinner parties thrown by our friends. As we arrived, I'd loudly announce, "Make way for King Arthur of Idaho! Also affectionately known as Sir Fish Breath!"

After all, we were mere peasants to him, and we lived to serve him. But never again in the guest bedroom. That only lasted for one night. We took great pride in spoiling him. Squie thought it was hilarious when Arthur climbed inside the refrigerator and helped himself to the lunch meat in the bottom drawers. Of course, it was served to his Royal Majesty on a plate while he sat on his throne.

Because of James's allergies, my sister gave Arthur regular baths. My beautiful blond sister is not what you'd call a cat lover, but she worshipped our self-confident, prideful longhaired gray king. He regularly accompanied her when she did errands, and she picked up fish sandwiches for him at the drive-through.

Squire sneezed constantly, his eyes watered nonstop, and he choked down allergy pills, but he didn't complain. This was terribly unlike him, as he made a big deal out of little cuts on his finger! But the Squire felt that our little king was worth the discomfort. I like to think that Arthur's final reign over the Squire's home was the happiest time of his life. It definitely was for me, but maybe not so much for Squie.

As our little king slowly faded away, we knew the time had come for him to leave us. His drippy-eyed foster father made a beautiful turkey dinner for his last meal. True to form, Sir Fish Breath growled as he was hand-fed small portions from his china plate.

Getting Goliath

James had always dreamed of living on a ranch in Wyoming. After his lovely estate sold, we moved an hour south of Jackson where there is no town, only a tiny post office and a gas station next to a big bar filled with ugly, crudely-mounted taxidermy. Once word got out that I'd moved there, a few people called to let me know

Goliath's mother

that there were some dogs near us that were being terribly neglected. The dogs were on an old rundown ranch. It was a scary-looking place strewn with broken-down, rusted junk. What was most disturbing was the unfinished deck without a railing on the second story of the house. That deck was covered with children's toys and a tricycle. There was nothing to stop the kids from falling a full story to the rocky ground below. But the strangest thing of all was a hand-dug moat filled with water around the house.

I asked around to see what I could find out about the people who lived there. The neighbors suspected they cooked meth. The owners of the ranch went to Alaska for a month each year and left five-gallon buckets of water and food in the barn for the dogs. Eventually the dogs wandered to the neighbors' houses and were taken in. I also heard that the man who lived there had bred his huge mastiff to a Great Dane to make some cash. Several other people told me that he kept a .22 caliber pistol shoved in his belt. It went off one day and shot him in his private parts. He sounded like a member of the low IQ club to me, maybe the founder of this area's chapter.

On the way to town one day, James and I drove past what I referred to as the meth ranch. I told him what I had heard about the dogs and added that children lived in that house. He warned me, "Stay far away from that dump." He said he'd call the sheriff to see what he could find out, but my mind was secretly set on another plan.

I wanted to buy the dogs and adopt them into homes where they would be cared for. The strange, haunting moat filled with dirty water, along with the rumors about the owner being a drug dealer who packed a pistol, led me straight to my bank's drive-through for some cash. I put on my Wrangler jeans before I drove over to the meth ranch in an attempt to blend in and look Western. Then I rehearsed my lines out loud and occasionally glanced in my mirror, saying in a strong but purely fake-confident voice, "How much for the puppies? What about the mother? Is she for sale?"

Who knew animal rescue would involve so much acting? I felt I had no choice but to play this part. I continued to rehearse and memorize my lines. I pulled into the driveway and parked. A shiver shot through my body when a massive two-hundred-pound black dog sauntered up to my SUV. As she made her way over to my truck, my heart pounded harder, but it slowed down when she wagged her tail and licked the BBQ sauce off my hand from the ribs I'd been eating. She slowly, almost caringly, escorted me to the front door.

I tried to steady my right hand, holding the wad of damp, sweaty bills. As if I was a yoga instructor in tights, I inhaled deeply and then exhaled slowly, and told myself to calm down: the guy didn't know what I knew about him. My lips whispered, "Oh yeah, Namaste, kumbaya, ready or not here I go." The door swung open before I could even knock. A rough-looking man stood in front of me, with greasy hair and an unshaven face, wearing a stained, old velour bathrobe and cowboy boots thickly covered in mud.

A lit cigarette hung from the corner of his mouth. "What the hell do you want?" The wooden handle of a pistol stuck out of the pocket of his bathrobe. Obviously, he was not too bright if he was packing again after his accident with the gun. The house reeked of trash, which I could see piled up as high as his knees throughout the first story. From upstairs, I heard faint voices of small children. The bottom floor of the house was despicable. I couldn't imagine what the top floor, where the children were, looked like.

My voice cracked when I said, "Heard you have some Dane puppies for sale."

"We had some, but they got run over. I think one of them got kicked by a mule out back. We got one left and I'm gonna keep him. He ain't for sale."

I said, "What about this one?" My hand rested on the two-hundred-pound black dog's head. "Is she the mother? She seems sweet. I would like to buy her."

He said, "She's not much of a watchdog. Nope, she's not for sale. I'm gonna have another litter and get some money out of her."

"I've got cash to buy her. I can't find a Dane or mastiff anywhere." I opened the palm of my hand and showed him my crumpled-up bills. "Are you sure?"

He tossed his cigarette on the ground and lit another one, and then blew the smoke in my face and snapped, "I said she ain't for sale. I can make a lot more money than that with a batch of pups." He curled his upper lip, which was covered in an unattractive Yosemite Sam mustache, and slammed the door in my face. Had I failed in my acting? I should have brought more cash.

My body trembled as the mother dog followed me to my car. I handed her some beef jerky from my pocket and told her, "Remember me, girl. I'll be back for you. If I take you now, I could get shot."

The next morning, we drove by the ranch and slowed down to look for the dogs. James put his hand on my knee. "Don't worry, babe, you're going to get them someday. I just know you are going to get them. I spoke with the sheriff. He knows we want them, so be patient. They have something big in the works. You can be assured the problem is being fully addressed."

He added, "The sheriff told me that the last time he pulled into their driveway, they fired a few shots at him and shot the lights off the top of his car."

I was fortunate nothing had happened to me. But I also knew that no sheriff would ever forgive or forget the lights being shot off his car, especially in Wyoming.

A few weeks later, on my morning drive to town, I approached the meth ranch and slowed down to catch a glimpse of the dogs. Behind the willows next to the road, something black suddenly darted out in front of me. I punched the brake with both feet and cranked the steering wheel with both hands, skidding sideways off the road onto the steep gravel shoulder. When the dust settled, a huge black puppy stood two feet from my front bumper.

This was no coincidence; it was my chance to get him. My hands shook as I ripped off my belt and slipped it around his neck. He had no choice—he was going with me. I begged him—and God—to help me as I grunted, pulled, and pushed his huge body into the backseat of my SUV.

I tried to catch my breath. Then I looked into the rearview mirror—the enormous dog's face was racked with terror. I tried to reassure him, "Don't worry, big guy. I'm your new friend," and handed him what was left of my breakfast burrito.

In one quick swallow, it was gone. As I pulled off the shoulder, he leaned toward me, put his chin on my head, and tried to keep his balance. His big, black, blubber lips draped over my head as slimy drool dripped onto my hair. He'd obviously never been in a car before. I stayed still and hoped he wouldn't get sick.

Once I was positive that we weren't being followed, I pulled off onto a dirt road next to a long row of trees beside a creek. I got out and dropped to my knees by the water. I dunked my head in the ice-cold water to rinse his saliva out of my hair, which only seemed to make it worse. As I raised my head, the chilling water ran down my neck. My head cleared of the fear of being caught, and I thanked God that my SUV hadn't rolled over, and that the puppy was tucked safely inside. Seeing him inside my car did not feel real, but more like a dream. The gooey interior of my SUV and my slime-covered hair snapped me back to reality. I couldn't wait to tell James and have him meet the big guy, and we headed home.

My childish, silly behavior over the years must have rubbed off on James because when the enormous pup got out of my car, he jumped up and down and said, "Oh my God, babe, he's beautiful! We're keeping him no matter what you say. I absolutely insist." He had grown up with a large fawn-colored Great Dane named General and had always hoped to get another big dog like him someday.

I said, "Well, you might change your mind when you hear what happened. You're not going to believe this one." I lifted my hand to show how it was shaking and said, "First, I need a drink to calm my nerves. A strong one, so pour it like you don't own it, please."

He paused long enough from fawning over the puppy to see the rough state I was in. "What happened to your hair? It looks terrible," he said with a look of disgust.

"Well, that's the least of my worries. Are you my self-appointed hairdresser? This is the dog from the meth ranch, the pup we've been looking for."

He stared blankly at me as my story unfolded, and then he slowly nodded. "Something like that could only happen to you. I mean really, Rebecca, only you. For some reason, I'm not surprised. You always seem to get what you wish for. You wanted those two dogs. Now you have one. Good job. You, my sweet Boo Boo, have real guts!"

I sighed. "Maybe it's guts, or maybe I'm just stubborn and downright stupid. You know the pistol-packing, bathrobe-wearing, suspected drug dealer is not far away. He could hurt us and our animals."

He agreed it was not safe to keep the dog; we needed to move the puppy as quickly as possible. Then in a little boy's voice he said, "I'm going to pretend like he's ours until he's adopted."

He did not know that on the first night of fostering an animal, I always pretended quietly to myself that I would keep them, especially after removing them from a bad situation. It was my way of kidding myself and allowing me to love them until my phone rang, begging me to help another animal.

That night, James wrapped himself under the blankets in his bed in a pathetic attempt to hide from the playful puppy who was more like a wild pony when he pulled the pillows off the bed and tossed them into the air. The pony wanted to wrestle. James did not. The enormous black dog planted his paw on his stomach and left a long string of slobber on his gelled hair and covered his pillows in gooey spit. He yelled through the white sheet, "Get him off of me!"

I jumped on top of the bed and giggled just as the wild pup knocked me down. I jumped back up and pretended to make a trumpet noise with my fingers, "Don ta da da, I do hereby proclaim his name to be Goliath, for he shall be a gentle giant of a dog."

James laughed under the covers and peered over the sheet just as Goliath slammed down on his chest. My laughter did not last long when my mind envisioned the pistol-packing guy in the velour bathrobe.

The next day, as I was driving past the hospital in Jackson where two of my previous neighbors worked, I remembered—like a brick hitting me square in the head—that they had mastiffs and worshipped the breed! Bingo! They also lived in a very remote area, far away from the meth ranch, without any neighbors close by.

The big giant landed well at his new home, although there was the occasional bullying from their black, male shar-pei mix. Whenever Goliath had had enough of the shar-pei's nonsense, he'd sit on top of him and pin him to the ground. Goliath grew so tall that he could rest his head on the kitchen counter, and like his mother, reached two hundred pounds. He took two car rides in his life: one to my house and one to his forever home. After that, his adoptive parents were never again able to get him into a vehicle; their vet had to travel to the house for his examinations.

A few weeks after he'd settled into his new home, James and I were on our way to Jackson. We slowed down by the meth ranch and looked for Goliath's mother. I counted two dozen official vehicles parked on the side of the highway. I pinched James's arm and yelled, "Pull over right now!"

We grabbed our birding binoculars and counted twenty men in bulletproof vests—a SWAT team—as they leaned against the old log cabins, their automatic weapons held tight against their chests with the barrels of their guns pointed to the sky. There were nine police cars, an ambulance, and eight sheriff's cars parked on the side of the road. James was right; the sheriff did have something big in the works—it was the Feds, the Bureau of Alcohol, Tobacco, and Firearms (ATF).

James had read my mind when he said, "Perfect, now we can get Goliath's mother." He acted as though he were the one arresting the villains as he hit his hands on the steering wheel, "Babe, they are going down! They're going to prison!"

He called the sheriff later that morning and learned that several arrests had been made. More than twenty illegal firearms, ammunition, drugs, and a taxidermy bald eagle had been seized. The children were taken in by protective services. The sheriff said we could take the dog, since there was no shelter located in the area.

Later that afternoon, we drove over with a cooked chicken and told the giant beast she could have it if she got into my SUV. She was calm, sweet, and not much of a watchdog. I reminded James that most dogs don't argue when it comes to roast chicken. I know I don't. Big pieces of greasy meat would comfort her, or at least distract her from loading into my car. No one had been killed or hurt. I never would have believed what had happened if we had not both seen it with our own eyes.

Goliath's mother looked confused and a bit unsure in the back of our vehicle. It was a miracle she had not been shot earlier that morning with all the guns there. Her owners had been hauled away while she watched, and she was left behind, alone. It was a terrible home, but it was the only one she knew. I hand-fed her pieces of chicken, and she slowly licked her big rubbery lips between bites. The carcass was picked bare before we got back home. It was a mere appetizer for this baby elephant of a dog.

She ended up with one of James's old leather belts for a collar, and a horse's lead rope as a leash. She appeared unfazed when she walked around the house and met all our animals. When we were with Goliath's mother, she was sedate, content, and affectionate. She was a perfect baby elephant. The one day we went to town and mistakenly left her alone indoors, we came home to find the front door hanging by a single screw. She sat on the front porch as if nothing had happened. She barked loudly and wiggled with joy when we pulled up. Her baseball bat of a tail wagged with such strength, she innocently chopped down some of my blooming daises.

The next time we left her, we put her in the biggest dog crate I owned, a silver Dodge minivan. I parked it in our shed where it was cool and gave her a large fresh bone to chew on. She decided to push out the side window, then climbed out and sat at the end of our long dirt driveway and waited for us to return. When we got home, she pranced around and play-bowed to me, then licked my hand. The dinosaur-sized bone didn't have one tooth mark on it. The side window laid on the ground, unbroken. Again, she acted as if nothing had happened. Our baby elephant was unable to be contained.

Less than a week later, a relative of the previous owner of the meth ranch called the AAC. He wanted Goliath's mom returned to the ranch, which he apparently now owned. The next call was from the sheriff, who informed us she would be in good hands, and we must return her. I never met the man who took her away from us. James insisted that, for my safety, he'd meet with him. James told me that the inside of the cab of his truck had trash piled up to the windows. He was an older guy in dirty clothes, supposedly the father of the guy in the bathrobe. We later heard that he had thrown his son under the bus to keep his own freedom. The pistol-packing bathrobe guy was sentenced to twenty years in federal prison.

The family members who moved onto the ranch removed all the junk from the yard. They also painted the house and put up a fence around the house. A week after our baby elephant was returned, I called the woman who had taken over the ranch and asked if things were okay with the big girl. I tentatively asked if we could please have her as our pet. The woman said she understood my concern for her and that, unlike her previous owners, she took great care of her animals, as if they were her children. She informed me that she had taken Goliath's mother to the vet to be spayed and vaccinated.

The saga of the meth ranch had come to an end. I often never know how things end for the animals I help, and that's hard for me. Sometimes, driving by the ranch, I would see Goliath's mother sitting on an oversized red dog bed behind a new fence that kept her off the highway, which gave me comfort. Occasionally I would see her wrestling with her new dog friend. Our oversized foster girl was able to stay safely in her home with a family that was finally committed to her care. When I first rescued her, never did I think she would be able to find love in the home where she had once been so neglected. That story still amazes me to this day.

Venus andApollo

Venus and Apollo

Our phone rang at the AAC. It was my good buddy, Parker. He said, "Hey darlin', listen up. I got some dogs that need to come your way. I'll tell you the rest when you get here."

Just as I hung up the phone, Linda walked in the back door. I said, "We need to pay Parker a visit. Looks like we are going on a road trip to Idaho!"

I ran out into the parking lot and yelled like a five-year-old, "Shotgun!" which forced Linda to drive. I was not fond of driving the old van I had bought years ago for $400 from a Kiwi visiting the States to go kayaking with Olaf. He had used it not only as his transportation but also as his home, sleeping on a scummy old futon during his kayaking trip in Wyoming. It smelled like old BO and, at forty-five miles per hour, it shimmied and veered dangerously. The key was broken off in the ignition, and without warning the passenger seat would flip backward. Being able to start it without a visible key, I named the van "the mystery machine."

Spending a few hours away from the Center with Linda was time I cherished. It was a chance for us to laugh, set goals, and solve problems without constantly being interrupted. With Linda, I can be as wild as I want. She normally laughs and encourages me to be silly so she can join in. On that particular ride, I repeatedly switched radio stations and looked for songs that I knew the words to, and sang loudly—off-key—into my hairbrush.

Finally, she said, "Cupcake, that's enough. Please knock it off!"

When we arrived at the shelter, Parker took us into his office. I grabbed a donut with sprinkles off his desk and jammed it into my mouth as if I were a wild, starved savage. He rolled his eyes at me, and then said, "You know, we think we've seen it all, but this one really takes the cake. So…there's a guy that's breeding German shepherds, and the idiot tied three of them together with baling twine. One's a female in heat, and the two others are unneutered males. It took me three days to catch them. They've been running all over the hills. But now we have a real problem, and that's why I called my favorite gals. The guy that owns them has his wife callin' here a couple times a day. I can hear him yelling in the background, 'You tell them we ain't gonna pay to get our dogs back!' He sounds like a real jerk. So, with that said, I want to move them over to your side of the hill where he can't find them." (By "over the hill," he meant over to Wyoming from Idaho.) "I know you gals will do right by them. There are only two dogs left. One of the males had such bad hip dysplasia and was hurt so badly, the vet had to send him to heaven."

Parker said, "Now you listen up when I tell you, they are a lot of dog, so let me load them for you." I was taken aback by their sheer beauty. These two beautiful German shepherds had probably spent their lives outside in a pen for the sole purpose of making puppies and money. This was no American Kennel Club—it was what I called our AKCC, the Almost Killed Canine Club or the Almost Killed Cat Club.

We thanked Parker for the call. As Linda backed out, I jumped out of the van and smashed my tight lips against his fat, sandpaper-like cheek, and left a few colored sprinkles on his collar from my donut. Parker slammed his fat hand on the hood of the van and laughed, "Now you get out of here!"

He repeatedly called us on the worst cases of abuse and neglect. He gave those animals a chance. We'd all grown fond of his sarcastic sense of humor, and spoiled him with bottles of Jack Daniels, candy, homemade cookies, and flowers we'd cut from our gardens for his wife. He blushed like a shy country boy when we handed him our gifts and hugged him. When he got sentimental, I fake-punched his pudgy gut or karate-chopped his fat neck with a loud, "Hi-Yah! Parker, take that!"

Without saying a word, Linda went straight for our usual burger drive-through next to the shelter. We did this for a few reasons. One, they were hungry. Two, it was a treat they loved. And three, it helped distract them if they were crated. Maybe the dogs liked me more because I handed them their first hamburger. They deserved to be happy, and I was usually famished.

Linda looked at me and raised her eyebrows, tilted her head, and let out a slight whistle as we pulled up. "Cupper, these guys are going to need a few dozen burgers to put some meat back on their bones."

Even though the dogs were underweight and filthy, they remained magnificent, majestic-looking creatures. Their gorgeous fur and strong, striking bodies reminded me of wolves. I said to Linda, "Looking at these two stunning creatures, it's quite obvious that dogs descended from wolves." (My theory is that pugs must have descended from little wild boars.) I rode sitting backward in the passenger seat, petting their beautiful heads, and feeding them little pieces of the hamburgers. Then I leaned over towards Linda and playfully yelled in her ear, "I have an announcement to make." I turned towards the shepherds, "Welcome to our club, my new friends. This is when your life gets good!" In an overdone, dumb-sounding accent, I said, "You ain't gonna be running all over the hills no more!"

Linda said they needed exceptional names. "How about Venus and Apollo, after the Greek gods?"

In my continued fake accent, I said, "Well, I'll be darned if that ain't the two perfect bestest names for these scruffy wolf dogs."

Halfway home, we stopped down a dirt road between the thousands of acres of open potato fields. The big black-and-tan male, Apollo—with satellite dish ears that could have tuned in Tokyo—dragged me across the dirt and plants. He pulled so hard that my shoulder dislocated. (It does that from time to time if it's pulled too hard, but it goes right back into place.) That's when I said to Linda, "They are way too much dog for us." We knew how to get them groomed and fattened up, how to take them to a vet and adopted into qualified homes. Dog training is not on my resume. This was a job for our good friend Vicki

O'Brien, better known as "Big Red." She was one of our best-kept secret weapons at the Center.

Vicki is a common, average name. While Vicki O'Brian was many things, average or common are not the words I would use to describe her. Overly confident is more fitting. Her extra-large stature, along with her long, red hair and eagerness to take on challenges, gave me the idea to rename her Big Red. Red was a bigger cow-dog fanatic than I was, had taught agility classes, and had competed in the ring. She had also fostered hundreds of our dogs that needed some training. I called her on my cell phone and said, "Once again, I am in over my head with two magnificent beasts."

She started to giggle. "Well, tell me something I don't know already! Come on over. You can drop them here on your way home. I'll see what I can do with them. Shepherds are extremely intelligent. Did you know that they're working dogs?"

She had her yard set up to keep dogs, with a high fence and a dog door that led into her mudroom. We pulled up to her small farm in Victor, Idaho, where she kept chickens and her rescued horses. Red walked over from the barn to greet us. Her big, round cheeks were flushed and pink from working in the sun. She smiled as she pulled out a few blades of hay intertwined in her long copper-colored hair. Her grin widened as she looked through the van windows. The dogs lunged and barked. She laughed. "What are you waiting for? I'm ready—turn them loose!"

I told her, "You open the door. That big knucklehead back there with the satellite dishes for ears dislocated my shoulder about an hour ago and dragged me through the potato fields." When she slid the side door open, both shepherds leapt straight into the air. Red grabbed both leashes, pulled on them, and told the dogs firmly, "Sit!" And by God, they did. Both the dogs sat calmly next to her. She said, "You can leave them here. It will be fun." Within an hour of her direction, they both walked calmly on a leash and responded to her basic commands to sit and stay.

Venus had light, tan-colored fur. She was easier to train than the meat-headed but handsome black-and-tan brute, Apollo, and ended up being adopted after just a few days by a fantastic woman who knew the breed and had been on our waiting list for a female shepherd.

Meanwhile, my boyfriend James had been planning our long-awaited, quick, little vacation to Las Vegas, where there would be no dogs, cats, volunteers, or vet appointments. He strictly instructed me that to have a real vacation my cell phone would be turned off. This was going to be a real break for me, one I hadn't had in years. He'd purchased tickets to several of the fantastic Cirque du Soleil shows and had made dinner reservations at several exclusive restaurants. Our five-star hotel with a high-end, luxurious spa awaited me, with scheduled massages and a manicure and pedicure. James was fully aware of the nonstop daily challenges at the Center and had asked Red to personally handle them while we were gone. If there was a true emergency, she could call his cell phone, but it had to be a matter of life or death.

When we finally arrived at the lovely hotel, we lay in two big lounge chairs next to the pool. I had dozed off for a few minutes when his phone rang. When his voice got louder, I opened one eye to see his face turn bright red. Fuming, he asked in a low voice, "Have you called the police?" My eyes squinted in the sun as I frantically reached for his phone. He pulled away, "Listen to me. Shut the place down. Lock the doors. Get the volunteers and Apollo out right now!"

He slapped his Blackberry phone into my open palm. It was Red. She said a new young volunteer over at the Idaho shelter had innocently told Apollo's previous owner that we had him at the adoption center in Jackson. When the owner called the Center, Red answered the phone. She told me, "He said if we didn't hand over his dogs that he would be coming over to kill someone." She had stayed calm on the phone, and then called James right away.

She said, "I'm so sorry, but I just had to call and let you know. I think this might be a life-or-death matter."

I said, "No worries. You did the right thing. You know I am there for you and the girls when there's a problem. Oh my God, hang on. I just got the perfect idea! I'll get right back to you."

I dug my phone out of my bag, turned it on, and looked through my contacts. It was Parker's number I needed.

He was out on patrol. His country music blasted over the speakers of his truck as he answered his phone. I told him about the call and the threat. He said, "I'll have none of that! I'm turning my rig around right now, darlin'. I just happen to know where that guy lives. I'm about ten minutes out. No one is going to hurt my girls. Sounds like he needs a good talking to."

I called Red back. "Well, now . . . the good news is Parker promised that he's personally going to take care of this."

She burst into laughter, "Oh man, I bet he will! Looks like good ole Parker just gave us another reason we can't live without him."

Parker was cocky when he called me back. "Let's just say I was able to change his mind. You can rest assured he ain't coming your way—I can promise you that, darlin'. Now you rest up and work on your tan and go see your fancy, half-naked shows."

Parker never fessed up about how he changed that guy's mind. But I do know that he kept our staff, volunteers, and Apollo safe from any harm. He also saved my long-awaited vacation. What a relief for me and our animals to have Big Red, James, and good ole Parker on our side.

Big Red

When my friend Vicki O'Brien encountered a problem, she never looked away; instead, she took it on as a challenge that she would win. She politely took no nonsense from inappropriate people or ill-mannered animals.

Vicki and I worked closely together in the early phases of the AAC. Together we faced nonstop challenges, including difficult people, untrained dogs, and countless programs that needed to be developed, written, and imple-

Vicki O'Brien, better known as Big Red

mented. Without Vicki, I would have given up. She always took on the issues that I didn't have the time or energy to deal with. Like I said, she didn't mind confrontations, whereas I hate them.

I loved to hide behind her back and say, "Don't mess with us, or you mess with Our Big Red!" It became our mantra at the Center. Red took the cats that refused their litter pans and made homes for them in her barn. When our computer crashed, she fixed it. When a difficult person caused trouble, she handled the confrontation with a subtle smirk on her face. Red's patience and expertise in training transformed our dogs that needed basic manners. Her undying dedication and skills saved hundreds of animals' lives. When she took on a project, she saw it through to the end and did her absolute best.

All our dogs at the AAC wear collars with identification tags with the Center's phone number engraved on it. A call came into the Center early one morning from a man who said he'd picked up a huge black-and-tan, male German shepherd that was running loose on the highway on Teton Pass, the road that connects Idaho and Wyoming. It was Apollo, Red's foster dog. He was miles from her home, and the call left me with a sick feeling that something was terribly wrong.

Ten minutes later my office manager called me and said that Red had been seriously injured in a car accident on Teton Pass. She was being transferred to a much larger hospital by helicopter. Hysterical, I ran across the parking lot to the real estate office where Linda was on floor duty. Linda had worked in hospitals for more than twenty years as a respiratory therapist. She dialed the hospital, handed me the phone, and said, "You have to tell them you're her sister. It's the only way we can find out what's going on. They will only release information to close family members."

I caught my breath and softly said, "Hello, this is Mary O'Brien. I'm Vicki O'Brien's sister. Please tell me where she is."

The hospital in Driggs, Idaho, is small, with a just a few beds, and the emergency room nurse said, "Hang on, ma'am. Let me patch you through to the pilot."

The pilot was winded. He hesitated and stuttered, "I'm so sorry, ma'am. We never put her on the plane. I am afraid to say, she died in the hospital."

I shrieked, "No! No! No! Why would you say that?"

His words destroyed my world. I smashed the phone on top of the desk. Linda slowly picked it up and put her hand on my back, while she spoke with the pilot. After she hung up, she reached her arms out to hug me. I pulled away and hoarsely shouted through my tears, "How could they make such a big mistake? What is wrong with that guy?"

I had to see Red. We were meeting for lunch in an hour. "Linda, we need to go to the hospital and find out what's really going on."

Linda looked frightened and horrified when she said, "Cupper, please try and calm down. I will drive you over now." She held my hand as I bawled uncontrollably, and mouthed, "We'll get to the bottom of this."

Terrified into a state of hysteria, I gasped for air between my wailing screams. Linda pulled her car over and said, "Cupper, breathe in and out." Her hand tightened around mine. She kissed it, and said, "I will stay with you. Look at me and breathe."

We arrived at the small hospital. My knees weakened when we walked past the big, black coroner's hearse that was parked at the side door. My mind and body were totally numb. Linda walked by my side and held on to me. It was as if I were in a different dimension from the rest of the world. Linda sat me down on a small chair inside and said, "Look at me Cupper. Wait here, and don't move."

Linda immediately went into her hospital mode; these kinds of accidents were something she knew all too well from her twenty-plus years of working in hospitals. She quietly spoke with the head nurse, who agreed to let us into the room with Vicki's body and instructed us that the sheet must stay over her body and face while we were in the room.

We went in together. I knelt on the floor and lay my head on Red's bruised hand and kissed it. In nothing more than a hissed murmur, I thanked her for all she'd done for me and for our animals at the Center. I promised her that we'd take extra-special care of her horses, cats, dogs, and chickens. I told her I'd call her family before the highway patrol made a visit to their homes. Once everything was said, Linda walked me out into the sunshine. It was March, and the melting snow left huge puddles of water in the black asphalt parking lot. I thought, Red will never see the grass grow green in her pasture again, or her horses, dogs, or cats whose lives she saved and loved. Her family will be crushed; her mother, devastated.

Nothing seemed real. It was as if I was in a horrible nightmare and unable to wake up. My mind tried to hold on to a small hope that, somehow, she was alive, even after seeing her lifeless body under the sheet. I just needed to wake up. This must be the way our minds work to keep us from losing them. It's called denial and shock. I know now that time takes away the hope. The reality of death slowly sinks in when we're finally able to accept what has happened.

Linda held my hand tightly on our way over to Red's house, as I stared ahead, stunned into a silent, catatonic state. My eyelids were swollen shut from my tears. Linda pulled me by the hand into Vicki's house. Then she had me lie down and put a bag of frozen peas over my eyes. She searched the house and found a piece of paper with Vicki's family's phone numbers on it. After a few rehearsals, I made the dreaded phone calls that changed the lives of Vicki's family forever. I called her brother Shawn first, and he drove straight to their mother's house and shared the life-altering news.

About six days before she was killed, Red and I had spent a few hours talking in her home. She was proud of her accomplishments and the life she had made for herself. At the time of her death, she was thirty-six. While she may have been single, she was never alone. She shared her life with twenty-three rescue animals and countless foster dogs. She cherished her animal family and slept with three dogs in her room and two cats in her bed every night. Her barn housed her chickens, cats, and the boarded horses that also paid part of her mortgage.

How could this happen to her, of all people? She had worked so hard to save the lives of homeless animals, and now they all were orphans.

Red was the one who had insisted that the AAC start a horse-rescue program. She did all the research, signing up more than twenty qualified people to foster horses on their properties and barns. She found our first horses at a well-known summer youth camp. Their horses were headed to the slaughterhouse when she made the call that saved their lives. Red then made the ten-hour drive, loaded them onto her horse trailer, and took them to her big barn.

Months after her death, her words from our last board meeting still echoed in my head. She had said, "We have to be ready for the next horses that will need our help. You know there will be more horses. It's just a matter of time."

It was mind-bending that the horses she desperately wanted to save would turn out to be *her* horses. Her mother, sister, and two brothers took her precious dogs and house cats. Kind neighbors took her chickens and barn cats. It took well over a year to place her horses into homes she would have approved of.

Red's legacy left hundreds of people in our valley with beautiful cats and dogs she had pulled from the euthanasia list at shelters. She trained and nursed many of the sick ones back to health. Her undying commitment and astonishing amount of incredibly hard work had given our group the strength we needed to succeed during our first two rocky years of operation.

Julie Martin adopted our first horse from Red. After Red's death, Julie and a group of her horse-loving friends created the nonprofit Hapi Trails Horse Rescue in Victor, Idaho. With the help of foster parents, volunteers, and donations, many beautiful horses, mules, and donkeys that would have otherwise perished, now thrive. I think we all know, deep down on some level, that none of us know how long we'll be here. If your pets should outlive you, making plans for them today will save them from entering a shelter. For the sake of your pets, please make written plans for your pets today.

Rescued pugs Willy, Jake, and Conner

The Pug Connection

I've been adamant over the years, telling hundreds of foster parents, "Never look directly into the eyes of a puppy or kitten." The spell they cast is so strong, it can be impossible to break without crushing your heart into tiny pieces.

Leave it to me to give unsolicited advice and then not take it for myself. I guess that's another bad trait to add to my list of things to work on.

A week after Vicki O'Brien's fatal car wreck, I drove to the boarding kennel she used in Driggs to pick up one of her foster dogs that had survived the crash. In the center of the grooming room sat a circular pen where little black puppies squirmed as they nursed next to their mother. I asked my friend Pam, who owns the kennel, "What kind of dogs are these? They look like tiny pigs crossed with monkeys."

It was as if I had never seen a puppy before when I looked directly into one's eyes, picked him up, and mauled him with tons of little kisses. I acted as though he were my long-lost child that had been ripped from my arms at birth. I zipped him inside my vest and his stinky, skunky, puppy breath broke through my overwhelming grief. I walked around the kennel with him for an hour before I finally put him back in his pen.

In the weeks following Red's accident, James did his best to take care of me. His concern grew as my body shrank and my pants fell to my ankles without a belt. My insomnia persisted, the circles under my eyes grew darker, and deep wrinkles covered my tired face. When I looked in the mirror, I barely recognized my face or what had become of the life I once knew. What would I do without Red?

James's concern gave him the opportunity to do what he does best: create rich and delicious meals. But the thought or smell of food left me queasy. One day, I refused yet another of his lovely meals, and lay face down on my wet, tear-soaked pillow while I replayed in my mind scenes of me and Red talking at her house. James came in and sat next to me, gently pulled back my hair, and asked, "Is there anything that's made you happy in the past few weeks?"

My mind went straight to the little black nugget and his skunk-like puppy breath. I sat up in bed quickly and asked, "Did you know that pugs can have black fur, as well as the fawn color?"

He said, "Babe, what does that have to do with anything? You're not making any sense."

I said in a rather bossy voice, "Now you listen to me, Squie. There's a pug puppy that looks like a baby black gorilla boarding at Pam's kennel. He's a runt and needs my care, or he may die."

James patted me on the shoulder, looked confused, walked away, and came back with a glass of water.

The next day, he called me at work. "There's an urgent matter we must discuss immediately. Please meet me at home as soon as possible."

My nerves were raw. Physically exhausted and emotionally fried to a crisp, I paced frantically up and down the driveway to stay awake and worried what the bad news might be.

He pulled up with a sneaky grin on his face. When I opened the truck door, he said, "Now reach into the front pocket of my coat."

With a weak voice, I blurted out, "If this is urgent, why are you smiling?" My hand reached in and felt soft, slick, velvety fur in his pocket. It was the scrawny, black, baby primate from Pam's boarding kennel that I had almost smothered to death in kisses.

My anxiety turned into tears of relief and happiness. James's face lit up when he said, "Red wanted you to have him. He's a gift from her. She sent him to you. He's the only thing that's made you happy since her death."

He took my hand, walked me into the house, and, once we were on the couch, casually pulled the baby from my arms. "He wants to be with his daddy for a minute." James perched the little guy on his shoulder, lay back on the sofa, and turned on a football game. "Look, babe, I finally have someone to watch sports with. He likes sports, just like his daddy!" He had no intention of letting me hold him. It was glaringly obvious to me that he was now under the overpowering spell of a tiny black pug puppy.

During the first year of this little magical creature's life, his paws rarely touched the ground. His given name was Anthony, but his father called him "Little Man." He was not my dog, but a little black prince I had to steal from the pug hog.

James bragged to anyone who would listen about how regal Anthony was. In James's eyes, Anthony was royalty. This treatment convinced Anthony early in life that he was exceptional in every way. Dozens of times a day, James's deep voice bellowed, "Babe, just look at him. Will you look at Little Man right now? He is by far the best-looking and most intelligent dog in this world."

A week after his arrival, I suggested that we change his name to "Look at Him." The powerful spell Little Man cast on me didn't come close to what happened to Mr. Bossy Pants. He was a different person altogether and actually became quite pleasant to be around, overflowing with adoration for his newfound monkey-like baby.

The nonstop silliness and crazed feeling of love that accompanied this little monkey of a dog was more than I could stand, and I wanted more. More pugs! One of my own, now that Anthony ruled James's life. It was as if he had drunk some strange energy drink laced with a drug that caused him to lose his mind over pugs!

He rarely shared Anthony with me, or with anyone else. When Little Man did anything wrong, James laughed as if it were the funniest thing he'd ever witnessed, for Little Man could do no wrong in his eyes.

James went out and bought a hat with a pug embroidered on it. Let me tell you, Mr. Fancy Pants didn't wear a hat unless it carried a yacht club logo. I am sure he didn't *really* find the hat attractive but instead wore it to antagonize me. He condescendingly taunted me, "I'm an unofficial doctor of pugs, a self-proclaimed pugologist." Most of the time, our friends and I went along with his antics because it was kind of funny.

Pug mugs suddenly appeared along with pug lamps and pug bumper stickers on our cars. I guess we're not all that unique, as millions of people worship this breed and flaunt it. It was as if we were in some kind of pug cult, or what I call "pro-pug people."

From all the stupidity and ridiculousness that came along with getting Little Man, all that mattered in the world was that James and I started rescuing pugs in need of help.

Finding a pug in Wyoming is a difficult task, especially one to rescue. Wyoming is not overrun with dog breeders: thanks to the harsh subzero winters that last more than half of the year, puppies can't be bred and caged outside in backyards like in California, Arizona, or Florida. We looked online for pugs abandoned at shelters that needed a home. James was retired, so he looked day and night while Anthony lounged on his lap as if it were his throne.

Shortly after Anthony graced us with his magnificent presence, we went to Petco. We began looking for a salesperson, with the little black prince riding inside his daddy's cashmere sweater and peering out from the top of his coat when offered a treat. James reminded me of an attention-starved child—he wanted everyone in the store to notice and admire Anthony.

Once we finally found a clerk, James cleared his throat and said in an exaggerated, somewhat condescending voice, "Excuse me, kind sir, but will you please direct me to the pug items you have for sale?" The salesclerk quietly led us to the books. James took a quick glance at *Pugs for Dummies* and tossed it into the cart, along with everything Little Man didn't turn up his nose at.

Once we were back at his car, James asked me to drive so he could read *Pugs for Dummies* out loud to me. That was a first! He had read dozens of menus to me—as he lives to eat—but he'd never read any part of a book to me or asked me to drive his precious car.

He said, "Babe, we need to know everything we can about these guys. I don't want to make a mistake and have Little Man pay for it." Well, he also wanted to hand-feed the dog every single treat we had bought for him.

My nose scrunched up, my lip curled, and I wondered when James had ever admitted he had made a mistake, let alone tried to avoid one by reading a book that had "for Dummies" in the title. He ate up every word in the book as if it were the most scrumptious sandwich he had ever eaten. As anyone who knows him can assure you, he has eaten countless sandwiches.

His strange behavior continued. One day a while later he said, "After reading that book, I know what true pug behavior is." But when Anthony did something that he hadn't read in his instruction manual, he'd say, "Now that is very un-pug like. Not true pug behavior." He continually teased me, "As a certified pugologist, my credentials speak loudly for themselves. Now allow me to teach you, so you may become a better parent to Anthony."

After one of his many attempts to irritate me with an especially long commentary on Anthony's behavior, I finally lost my cool. "Come on, you're like the Bob Costas of pug behavior, giving me a blow-by-blow of Little Man sneezing, sleeping, begging, even eating! It has got to stop. I can't take it anymore; you're driving not only me but also the dogs insane! If you were actually funny like Charles Barkley or Shaquille O'Neal I wouldn't mind."

That's when he took my hand and said, "Well, I guess you don't know who you are dealing with! You just might learn something about this magnificent breed, if you cared to observe the little prince and his master—for I am now the true master of the pug language."

Once we became *those people*, preoccupied with pugs, our dedication to the breed trickled down to more than a dozen pugs we temporarily fostered and placed into overqualified, borderline-fanatical homes. We were also able to provide a final home and hospice care for older pugs at the end of their lives. You must also know, the self-proclaimed pugologist always tried to adopt every one of them, which I never allowed.

It has been well over a decade since James and I have been together, but our silly love for these dogs has never been broken. Little Man continues to sit on Daddy's lap as if it is his throne, like a self-righteous Little Lord Fauntleroy. Of course, the doctor of pugs still laughs and stares at him more adoringly than anything else in his life. When he calls me to say, "Babe, look at him. I mean would you just look at him?" I laugh, of course, and picture Anthony in my mind to humor the man who may love these pugs more than me.

Gabriella

Gabriella

For me, as the executive director of a nonprofit, every day was a workday, and holidays held no real meaning. My responsibilities forced me to be behind a desk, or on a computer or the phone. My favorite thing in life is pulling animals out of shelters, and that task had been delegated to my staff.

Once again, we had run out of animals at the AAC. On this particular day, which also happened to be the Fourth of July, I insisted that I drive to the shelter alone. On the way, my phone rang, and an unfamiliar voice with a country twang said, "Hello, ma'am, I am an animal control officer over here in Idaho. I work with your friend Parker. He gave me your number and told me I had to call you personally. About a month ago a couple of kids found this dog in a field with a pretty bad gunshot wound. They hid her from their landlord in their apartment. Now her leg is really bad and needs to come off." He hesitated. "You know I'm not real sure, but she might already be too far gone."

I said, "If you can believe this, I am on my way over there right now, only about ten minutes away."

His voice picked up, "Well, all right then. She's some kind of patchy-colored cow dog, a real nice girl, for all she's been through, with some real sweet eyes. About a year old, and I'd say a blue merle-Aussie mix."

I asked, "Which vet is on call over there this weekend?"

He hesitated, "Well, now, that ain't good news. It's old Doc Pierre."

I said, "Thanks for calling. Please tell her to hang on. I'm almost there." My fast talking might not convince this vet to help her. He was the one who put the animals to sleep at the shelter, and never appeared to like either cats or dogs.

I hung up and immediately dialed his number. With a firm but polite voice, I said, "Good morning, Dr. Pierre. I have an emergency and need your help. My dog needs her back leg amputated; I happen to be visiting Idaho Falls right now."

He stammered and then got snippy, "I'm closed and headed out now to a family picnic. Call me Monday."

I said, "Aren't you the emergency vet on call for the city this weekend?"

He interrupted, "Well, I know who you are. I only take care of owned dogs, and by that, I mean my paying patients on the weekends. Not shelter animals."

"Oh . . . she's mine, I adopted her. I also have cash to pay you today." It was the cash from James's dresser. He'd leave money in an envelope for me on days I pulled animals from shelters. I never asked for it. He called it the green handshake money. As James said, "Few can resist a wad of cash." When I'd put it in my pocket that morning, I'd felt guilty, but I'd taken it anyway.

When I arrived, the nice officer I'd spoken with took me to the poor dog, who was too weak to lift her head. I squatted down next to her in her kennel, and she barely lifted her tail off the floor. Her back leg was a matted mess of dried blood that stank like rotten meat. Her pretty patches of speckled, puffy fur reeked of cigarettes. I gagged and whispered, "Don't worry, girl, you're going to make it. Hang on." Her body stayed limp when I scooped her into my arms.

The officer was a sweet, young, country boy with big, round, brown eyes and a full, round face. His blue polyester uniform was stretched tight over his large stomach. He said, "Well, now, I was gonna carry her; at least let me get the door for ya."

Grunting I asked, "So are you here all day? I want to come back for some more cats and dogs."

"Yes, ma'am, I'll be here. You can just come in the back door. Parker said you take the bad cases. Can't believe you got old Doc Pierre to meet you. You must have some kind of magic; he's an ornery old coot."

My heart beat faster when I stepped on the gas to make a yellow light. I said out loud to myself, "Stay calm and be nice. Don't be too pushy." I reminded myself that no matter how frantic I felt, that wouldn't save her. I took a few deep breaths and said, "Stay nice. Stay strong. God, please help her live—only you can save her."

I pulled in and parked next to Doc Pierre, who leaned against a shiny new Suburban. His stern-looking, unfriendly wife sat in the driver's seat and scowled when I cheerfully and insincerely greeted them. "Thanks for meeting me." His wife's painted-on eyebrows formed a severe arch, which made her appear as though she could pull a gun from her purse and start shooting. Her sprayed-stiff hairstyle and demeanor reminded me of Nurse Ratched from the famous movie *One Flew over the Cuckoo's Nest* with Jack Nicholson. I mean really, who didn't hate *her* guts?

I grabbed the green handshake envelope off the front seat and handed it to him through my window. He took a quick glance inside, and then stuffed it into his back pocket and whined, "Oh, all right, let's get this done. My grandkids are waiting on me at the lake with our boat. You know you're wasting your money on a shelter dog."

For decades, he and his wife had been putting thousands of animals to sleep in that shelter. Maybe that's how he and Nurse Ratched got to sleep every night, both convinced that shelter animals had no value. She shot me a quick glare before she sped away on the scalding, sticky asphalt, and her tires squealed. I said under my breath, "My, my, Nurse Ratched, what a lead foot you have."

The wretched odor of the dog's dead leg hung heavy in the room. I kept my nasal passages closed and breathed through my mouth. I averted my eyes from her bad leg as I placed her on the chilly metal table. I stared at the clock on the wall, trying to distract myself from the cuts being made with the scalpel. I snapped out of my daze when the vet snarled, "Grab her leg and bag it." I tried to act like I'd done this a thousand times. I felt nauseated, weak, and dizzy.

In the rescue world, this is called working in the trenches, on the frontlines. It is no place for crybabies. It's where tough decisions are made using logic, not emotions, where people try to do the right thing to protect beings unable to speak for themselves.

I stood in a trance, breathing through my dry mouth, and felt myself slightly swaying back and forth. His voice snapped, "That's all I can do for now. The bullet left bone shards embedded in her back hip. Once they work to the surface, she'll need another surgery to remove them, and that's going to cost you more money."

As if he were my commanding officer, I blurted out, "Yes, sir, I understand."

"I'll swing back to check on her after the fireworks and call you in the morning. Drop the garbage bag in the dumpster on your way out," he ordered.

My toes were exposed in open flip-flops, and when the black plastic bag that held her removed leg grazed them, chills shot up my own leg.

It was a relief knowing that medicine flowed through her veins that would rid her of the infection that ravaged her body. I placed the sleeping patient carefully in her kennel and whispered, "Don't give up, girl; you're going to get better. I'll come back and get you." My eyes shut as my lips kissed her freckled cheek.

I drove with my head halfway out the window on my way back to the shelter, hoping the blowing air would wipe my mind clean of what I had witnessed with this beautiful dog's severe injury.

I whipped open the back door of the shelter, and the sweet officer smiled and asked, "How'd it go? Did she make it?"

I said, "He amputated her leg and she's on antibiotics. So far so good."

"Well, I'm surprised you got that old codger to do anything. He's one ornery fella. Lucky for her you were so close when I called. Kind of strange, don't ya think?"

Maybe to him, but not to me. Coincidences reinforced my conviction that I was on the right path.

Krissy, my enthusiastic, upbeat colleague at the Center, called my cell phone. "Hey, Cuppers. I talked to a real nice guy at the shelter. Did you get the dog with the bad leg?"

"Yeah, it's done. I got her to the vet and had the pleasure of holding her leg while he sawed it off."

Her voice sang slightly when she spoke, "Aah . . . well, that's great news! I decided to name him Gabriel after the angel."

I interjected, "He's actually she."

She laughed. "Okay, then Gabriella it is! Now listen, Cuppers, don't worry; she'll make it. We all know the perfect family will adopt her. Everyone here is rooting for her, and we can't wait to meet her. This was so meant to be! Get as many animals as you can. We've got many great people here waiting for cats and dogs." She ended with her usual loud, happy voice, "Well, good work! And for God's sake, carry on! I've filled out Gabriella's medical chart because I know she's going to make it."

The next morning, crabby Doc Pierre called. He grumbled, "You can come and get her. Her temp has dropped considerably and she's ready to go. I will require the rest of the payment today."

To show respect, I quickly answered, "Yes, sir." Before I could thank him, he hung up without saying goodbye. I ran through the house, dancing and yelling, "Gabriella made it! She is coming home to us! Yay!" I jumped up and down, kissed the faces of the five dogs I had adopted over the past year, and spiked a pillow off the couch onto the floor.

I put extra rugs down on the living room floor, and James made a lovely bed for us on the floor next to the fireplace. Once again, he was the perfect host to our new, three-legged foster dog. On my way to pick her up, I purchased a rubber dog boot to put on her remaining back paw for extra traction.

Gabby was upright in her kennel when I peered in the door, and the loud banging of her tail against the metal kennel wall showed me she was stronger. She had a look of anticipation in her eyes and seemed to smile when I opened her cage.

As I spoke to her on our way home, she looked at me in the rearview mirror. She was so pretty and starved for attention that she reached with her paw for my hand to keep petting her. Looking in the rearview mirror as I drove, I saw her tilt her head when I spoke to her.

Gabby did far more for me than I was able to do for her. She soothed my raw nerves when we slept side by side on the mattress on the floor at James's house. She reminded me how vital it was to be there for injured animals like her that needed my help. Up until this point, I had always made a conscious effort not to get too emotionally attached to the animals, which saved me from more tears and protected my overly sensitive heart. With Gabby, though, I did not fight my feelings, and loved her completely from the moment I picked her up off the floor at the shelter. Maybe my guard was down because things weren't going well with James. I wasn't surprised—I knew we didn't have enough in common to stay together. We had been together for almost two years, and had supported each other through some difficult times in our lives. Without Little Man and our other lovely animals, it would have ended much sooner. While I would miss our time together with the dogs and James's fun-loving friends, the time was getting closer for me to move back permanently into the little bunker I rented up in the woods, good old Camp Chickamunga.

Gabby was healing quickly, so I decided to leave her at the Center one day when I had a meeting in town. My two top girls, Amanda and Krystal, begged to babysit her. They knew how to protect her from the mobs of animal-loving tourists who gave our cats and dogs almost too much affection during our busy summer months.

The girls were instructed to make a special hospital room using bedsheets as curtains for privacy in one of our dog apartments, with a polite sign asking people to stay away. They dragged a large neon poster board into the office and, using a stinky King-Kong-sized black magic marker, wrote, "Shooooosh!!!! Please be quiet and don't look in here! This is an ICU for a hurt dog. Sorry, but no petting allowed!"

Once they finished the sign, they marched back into the office with clipboards under their arms that held special charts with Gabby's photo. As she flipped over the papers, Krystal said (she was probably around ten years old at the time), "Now, Amanda and I are going to test and see what types of bones, food, and treats Gabby likes the best, if she feels up to it. We'll chart her progress on these forms we made especially for her."

I said, "You mean a taste test? Will she be blindfolded? That may look strange—a dog missing a leg, bandaged up, and blindfolded? She won't look like your patient, she'll look like your hostage, so don't forget to keep the privacy curtain up." I threw some papers into the air. "I can retire now that we know you two can run the show! Your detailed charts are impressive and that, my friends, is why you are the best dynamic duo here at the Center, in training to soon become the new executive directors. If only you were old enough to legally drive, I could quit now."

Martha, my perfectionist office manager at the time, was running the office that day. She used extra caution with our sick and injured animals. I trusted Martha with my life. She also corrected the girls when they used improper grammar and occasionally gave them each a dollar when they used a new word to expand their vocabulary.

The kids set up what I referred to as the "Monet Suite." A reproduction poster of Claude Monet's *Water Lilies* hung in a cheap gilded frame with dark rich paisley sheets sewn into valances around the edges of the kennels. This was my silly way of trying to make it more like a home, not a shelter. I knew the frame was garish and never would have allowed it in my house, but our dogs did not care.

My parting words were, "Now I trust all of you to prevent any serious mauling of your hostage. I mean your patient. Make sure Gabby gets plenty of affection and rest so she can continue to heal."

Martha said, "Get out of here before you're late. The girls know what to do."

During the meeting, my mind drifted back to Gabby, the girls, their sign, and her makeshift hospital room. I was grateful for Gabby's recovery, Martha's extreme attention to detail, our girls whom we all loved, and our unbelievable staff and volunteers who made our rescue work possible. More than anything, I loved the animals receiving the help they needed from our family at the Center.

The formalities of running a nonprofit bored me. I wanted to run with the dogs, play with the kids, and hang out with the cats in Kitty City. Anxious to return to Gabby, I counted down the minutes on my watch, kept my comments to myself, nodded my head and raised my eyebrows at the appropriate times, and then skipped lunch to get back to Gabby.

When I opened the back door to our dog apartments, the privacy curtain was on the floor, the Monet Suite door was open, and the ICU sign hung sideways on a thin strand of tape. Gabby lay wedged on a dog bed between a lovely woman and a handsome man in golf clothes.

The blinding glare of the woman's huge diamond ring screamed, "*We have money!*" The man gently stroked the fur on Gabby's back as the woman affectionately caressed her head. Gabby barely glanced at me; she looked directly at them when they spoke. We'd seen this hundreds of times. Gabby had chosen them to take her home.

Martha pulled at the back of my shirt and walked me into our office. Confused and frightened, I asked, "Why are those people making a Gabby sandwich?"

She quickly shut down my rant, "Now, Cupcake, hold up one second. Listen to what I have to say first. They're from California. She's a trauma nurse who works part time in the ER and deals with gunshot wounds. Her husband is a plastic surgeon in Brentwood. They were extremely curious when they saw the ICU sign and begged me to meet Gabby. I told them they could take a glance at her leg since they were professional medical people."

Blindsided, my stomach felt hollow with a twinge of nausea. Krissy's gleeful voice came to mind, "The perfect family will adopt her." My eyes suddenly burned, because Gabby was ready, but I wasn't. I had wanted Gabby to be my dog. I knew it was over between James and me, and soon I'd be moving out and renting again. I knew better than to start adopting too many dogs as a renter in a town that so rarely has rentals available.

I didn't want to spend my entire life as a blithering idiot in tears, so I switched gears and went into my Kevin Hart stand-up routine. Like the Seinfeld show, we had a lot of inside jokes. Our strange language at the Center was a series of inside stories that we called Cupcakeisms. I stood up, went over to Martha, and whispered in her ear, "Well, did you actually look at their resumes before you handed her over? For God's sake, I thought you could do better than that!" I then leaned over and gave her a smooch on the top of her head.

After I started to get over being dumped by Gabby, I went back in the room, sat on the floor next to them, and introduced myself. They apologized profusely for disregarding the instructions on the sign. Gabby took a quick look over her shoulder at me. I was hurt to see my patient so taken with them, her head resting contently on the woman's thigh. She didn't need me to pet her anymore. Her body was being massaged by their four eager hands. Gabby was breaking up with all of us at the Center (a Cupcakeism). I casually and quickly wiped my eyes. "Were you looking to adopt a dog, or were you stopping in to pet them? After all, we are an unofficial petting zoo."

The woman gave me such a big smile that her big, white, perfect teeth almost blinded me. I suspected they were veneered or crowned—there was no way they were real. Her complexion was also completely unblemished. I became jealous and felt rather haggard compared to this *Town & Country* couple.

"Well, it's so interesting. Right as we walked in the door, we'd agreed only to adopt a dog if we received a sign that it was the right dog for us."

Suddenly I felt a chill. "Bet you didn't know the sign would damage your eyes with the blaring pink neon. So, when you don't follow the rules here, you have what we call some making up to do. Kind of like a penance without the confessional or religion attached."

Krystal said, "Yeah, if you buy a dog or a cat instead of adopting one, you automatically receive twenty hours of volunteer makeup time here."

"We need to know if you're qualified to adopt her, although my real fear is that you're both overqualified; otherwise, Martha wouldn't have granted you permission to examine her." I casually but carefully studied the attractive plastic surgeon's face and wondered if his flawless features had been surgically altered by a coworker.

Our precious, skilled dog wrangler Amanda looked nervous when she handed me the adoption form they'd filled out in impeccable penmanship, and whispered, "Sorry, Cuppers."

The handsome doctor cheerfully asked, "What's next in the process?"

I cleared my throat and said, "Let's get down to business, since Gabby has tossed us to the curb like a burnt match. First, we could waive her adoption fee and trade straight up for my long overdue facelift." I then turned to his exquisite wife. "I have no real enemies, so a gunshot wound is probably not in my near future. Your skills will be of no help to me, but Gabby will need them to continue her recovery. You could also be of great help if you donated your King-Kong-sized diamond ring to pay off our vet bills. We'll happily replace it with brand-new cubic zirconium, and no one will ever know. After all, what happens in Jackson stays in Jackson, especially at the adoption center."

The attractive, well-groomed woman completely ignored my request and said, "We understand her medical issues and are committed to providing her with whatever is necessary for her to make a full recovery. We have the financial resources."

Then her husband looked at his phone. "Honey, excuse me, I need to cancel my tee time with the boys." A well-educated, successful, gorgeous man was canceling his golf game to be with a three-legged injured mutt. He was definitely over-overqualified.

Gabby barely glanced my way when I asked, "So, pretty baby, do you want to go with them?" Instead, she tilted her head, wagged her tail, and stared directly into the eyes of her new mother, a genuine certified nurse who was probably also a former Miss America. Our job was finished. I felt a slight pain in my heart. The tears that welled in my eyes were happiness for her and sadness for me.

The girls pulled out the red wagon we kept for our injured dogs. They'd padded it with pillows and blankets. Krystal said, "I used the nice ones since she'll be staying at the Four Seasons."

I'm ashamed to admit that, for a split second, I was overtaken with jealousy that she'd have twenty-four-hours-a-day room service available at her new temporary hotel home. (Yes, I am that shallow that I was jealous of an injured dog.)

Gabby was pulled into the Four Seasons resort in our red wagon, where dogs are not smuggled in, but welcomed by a bellman. A world-famous five-star hotel was an enormous upgrade from the silly Monet Suite with the gaudy cheap print. Her new parents canceled their flight home and rented a large, red Cadillac Escalade to take their new baby back home to California.

One Who Stands Alone: Dr. Heather Carleton

Heather Carleton, DVM

After four years running the Animal Adoption Center, my life in Jackson was getting difficult. My relationship with James had come to an end, and my workload at the AAC was growing on pace with our success in adoptions. I cried more easily and slept less every night, which only made me crazier than normal. I was short on patience. Simply put, I was burnt out—fried to a crisp.

We advertised both locally and nationally to find someone to replace me, but with no luck. And it wasn't just me who needed a change. No matter what Linda said, I knew she was worn out from the demands I placed on her. She started looking at properties in Colorado; Jackson had gotten too rich for her. I felt the same and wanted out, but unlike me, she was free to leave her ex-husband, the Center, me, and Jackson behind. I felt like a wild animal caught in a leg-hold trap, unable to move until my replacement could be found. My lack of freedom, and self-pity, turned me into a whiny martyr and I was absolutely miserable to be around. I wanted my life and freedom back, and desperately wanted to run away with Linda to Colorado and have fun again.

But before either of us could go anywhere, we had one major goal still to accomplish: implementing a low-cost spay and neuter program. Linda and I knew that to stop animals from entering shelters they must never be born in the first place. To stop them from being born, communities needed to provide free or low-cost spay and neuter programs so people could afford to have their pet fixed.

Toward the end of my four-year reign as the executive director of the Center, an articulate, well-educated woman came into the AAC and asked if we could go outside and talk for a few minutes. She introduced herself as Dr. Heather Carleton, and said, "I'm interested in helping your organization. I understand your mission and what you're doing here to save lives. I have a plan to implement affordable spay and neuter clinics throughout Wyoming." She went on to say, "I volunteered in Thailand doing spay and neuter clinics with the group Soi Dog, and during that time, I realized that Thailand, a developing country, was doing more to prevent pet overpopulation than we're currently doing in Wyoming." I knew right away that she was one of us.

Creating a program as monumental as what she envisioned took a serious commitment, and she succeeded. She sacrificed her personal life for several years, and demonstrated relentless determination in gathering equipment and staff, scheduling and advertising the clinics, and writing the grants to fund them.

In her persistence for the program to succeed, Dr. Carleton met with the Tribal Councils of Indian Reservations and veterinarians throughout the state. She advertised the clinics, found locations, and gathered veterinary technicians who drove long distances across the state, sometimes in treacherous weather, to help.

Dr. Carleton's mother, Mary, joined the group of hardworking animal lovers. One of her many jobs was to help animals recover as they awoke from anesthesia. This was a tiring job, working on hands and knees for twelve hours a day, helping more than one hundred recovering animals each day. Mary also followed up with each pet owner the day after the surgery. Homeless animals brought to these clinics from the Indian reservations were taken to the Animal Adoption Center in Jackson and put up for adoption.

When I asked Dr. Heather what her biggest challenge was in starting the program, she said, "Finding at least one vet in each town to sign on as a follow-up doctor for the animals that have been to the clinics. At least half of the vets didn't even want to speak to me. They said I was stealing their patients."

Nothing could have been further from the truth. No vet was offering free or low-cost spay and neuter surgeries in Wyoming. Despite the lack of support, Dr. Carleton continued her intense focus on her mission and did not give up. Within the second year, many of the veterinarians realized she was not going away and contacted her, agreeing to be the attending doctor for her spay and neuter clients. To date, more than twelve thousand cats and dogs have been sterilized throughout the state under the Wyoming Spay-Neuter Program established by Dr. Carleton.[2]

It was shortly after Dr. Carleton had established spay and neuter clinics that Linda moved to Colorado. But she wasn't gone for good. She came back to help, and together we volunteered at a clinic held on the Wind River Reservation. We witnessed firsthand how hard the staff worked as they lifted heavy dogs, drained and cleaned their wounds, trimmed their nails, and shaved animals in preparation for surgery. They worked on their feet for a minimum of twelve hours without one single complaint and gave every animal the excellent care they deserved.

While we were there, a man brought in four dogs. When I thanked him for bringing in his dogs, he responded, "You know, I'm sick of

2   Visit animaladoptioncenter.org for more information on the spay and neuter program of Wyoming

shooting puppies. I don't want to shoot them—and won't if I don't have to." We met a kind woman who fed feral cats and was incredibly grateful for the clinics. She trapped five cats and brought them in to be fixed one Saturday. When I asked if she had more cats she could trap and bring the following day, she shyly answered, "Yes, there are so many more, but I can't catch them all or feed them all." The next morning, she had eight more cats for surgery. She was obviously upset when she said, "The cats just keep showing up, more and more every month. Some of them are sick, and many have died."

Later, we loaded the cats into her car and added several large bags of cat food we'd bought for her. The woman looked bewildered, "And now you give me food? How did we get you people to come? How did you know we needed help? You must be sent by God." I genuinely believe that Dr. Heather and her team were. With tears brimming from our eyes, Linda and I hugged the woman tightly. She was also one of us, but lived in a bleak, dismal area and felt hopeless. She whispered, "God bless you. Thank you for helping the animals here." It was a humbling, beautiful experience in my life, one that stands clear in my mind.

In 2016, Dr. Heather Carleton was named Citizen of the Year by the Jackson Hole Chamber of Commerce for her efforts to help animals and for her work on the Wind River Reservation, which helped both residents and pets in need. In 2017, she received Employer of the Year from CES, a local nonprofit that helps improve the lives of individuals with disabilities. I am extremely proud to know her and to call her my friend.

Ms. Little

Ms. Little

After what felt like an eternity, but in reality was only four years, I stepped down as the executive director of the Animal Adoption Center. After several months of rest, I regained my strength and returned to my other chosen purpose in life: providing care for the elderly, disabled, and hospice patients in their homes. I continued fostering for the AAC, and one day they called me to take a senior Pomeranian who was neglected and quite ill. I was more than happy to help, especially since they'd be paying her vet bill.

The volunteer who drove her over to my house knocked on my door and said, "Wait till you see her. She's the most precious little animal I have ever laid eyes on. I just want to squeeze her she's so stinking cute. Good thing you're taking her. The poor little baby is pretty sick."

I looked inside the car where a tiny, red, six-pound Pomeranian was wrapped in a baby blanket, coughing and trembling. Her little brown eyes welled with tears when I picked her up. She was fragile, sick, and incredibly frightened. Her owner hadn't cared for her fluffy red coat, and she'd been shaved down to the skin and given a lion cut—her head was surrounded by a full mane, and her back was shaved clean with a little tuft remaining on the end of her tail.

She didn't look like a dog—she looked more like an expensive stuffed toy for a child. When she curled her lip and growled at me, I noticed that the few teeth she had were crusted in green and brown tartar. No one had told me that she also had rotten teeth. I said, "My God, you're one little teeny-weenie precious peanut. How would you like to be called Ms. Little?"

Ms. Little had been placed in one of the drop boxes on the side of the shelter building. People use the boxes when the shelter is closed to avoid paying the surrender fee. The drop boxes serve a purpose and stop people from leaving animals on the side of the road. Made of poured concrete, the boxes have a thick metal door on the outside and one on the inside of the shelter, kind of like a bank drop box. Once the animal is placed inside and the outside door is shut, it locks. The drop boxes are not heated, and there is no food or water. Over the years, I've seen all kinds of animals placed in these boxes: mother dogs with puppies, cats with kittens, and many purebred dogs. I've also seen pathetic older animals like Ms. Little, with matted fur and rotten teeth, whose owners are no longer able or willing to care for them.

Back then a dental treatment for a dog or cat could cost between $300 and $1,200, which was often a deal breaker for a rescue group struggling for funding. When animal shelters lack space, the best chance for the animals' survival is to put them into foster homes or transfer them to a shelter with space and funding. I was extremely grateful for the opportunity to help save Ms. Little's life. My help meant getting her through her sickness with antibiotics, patience, and supervision.

Anyone who looked at her did a double-take and then smiled. I wanted to mush her with kisses but clenched my teeth and restrained myself. She needed to come to me on her own terms, and earning her trust was going to take some time. When she did finally sit on my lap, I felt quite privileged and soon, overprotective.

Ms. Little was not friendly and snapped at everyone who looked sideways at her. After my vet Theo removed her few remaining rotten teeth, she was completely harmless. There were several people who were interested in adopting her, but she was not interested in them. My last-ditch effort to place her in a great home was when my mother came for a visit. I was elated; this would be the perfect match. I envisioned my mother as she waved goodbye, and they boarded the plane together.

As I mentioned earlier, Ms. Little was often snippy with other people, but when my mother arrived, she was downright vicious. She repeatedly gummed at my mother's face, hands, and even her shoes! Maybe she knew that I was attempting to match her with my mother.

Teeth or no teeth, there is no snapping—at dogs or at people—allowed in my house. Ms. Little spent most of my mother's visit in her crate gumming her bone with one eye on my mother.

At the time I had four dogs in my pack. If I were to keep Ms. Little, it would be five. But given her size, it would have been more like having four-and-a-half dogs. A temperamental, toothless Pomeranian—a teeny-weeny red lion—was not my idea of a real dog. But you know what? I kept her anyway.

My friends and I spent a lot of time working to break her ugly gumming behavior. Now she sits on people's feet and waits for them to bend over so she can launch herself straight into their arms. Her once-terrified face beams with confidence, shining for those of us lucky enough to be graced with her magical, toy-like presence.

I'm never sure who will adopt my foster dogs, but this time, I am happy she chose me. Ms. Little taught me that no matter the size, breed, or grooming of a dog, I love them all.

Drop boxes on the side of the shelter where Ms. Little was abandoned

Conner, Henry Thomas, Grace, Trixie, and Ms. Little

The Hitchhiker

Although I wasn't personally involved, this rescue story is too good not to share, and it's no coincidence that I heard it. It is a wild story of a cat that needed help and received it from a gorgeous ski bum.

It was the dead of winter in Jackson. With one major snow dump after another, the snowbanks on the sides of the roads were over four feet high. I turned onto the road that ends at Jackson's ski area, Teton Village, and noticed a guy with his thumb out. He had a pair of skis balanced on his shoulder. He looked like a ski bum, not a serial killer, so I slowed down, rolled down my window, and asked him, "Hey, do you like animals?"

"Yeah, I love them. Why?"

I said, "Okay, you can get in."

He carefully slid his skis in between all the dogs in the back and dropped into the passenger seat with a huge smile. I felt super self-conscious—this guy was exceptionally handsome. He had shiny dark brown hair and a perfectly tanned face, along with a sexy smile and perfectly shaped, blindingly white teeth. I could tell by the look on his face that this guy knew he was way above average in the looks department. From the ski goggle tan lines on his face and the full-season ski pass around his neck, it was obvious he lived to ski—nothing unique in this valley.

My black pug, Connor, jumped onto his lap and licked his face. Trixie, my border collie, reached her head over, put her chin on his shoulder, and pushed down from the backseat, letting him know he was in her spot. Ms. Little, my itty-bitty red Pomeranian, let out a tiny "grrrrrrr."

He laughed. "Oh man, how many dogs do you have?"

I proudly answered, "Five dogs, but with all of the animals I rescue, there are usually a few foster dogs, too."

"Wow, they're all awesome and get along so well. Is this a black pug? Man, what a cool little dude."

I said, "Yeah, Connor has been known to lick the felt off a tennis ball, so you can say goodbye to any sunblock you applied this morning."

In my back seat there was my rez dog Grace, who looked like a dried-up old wolf; Connor, a dead ringer for Danny DeVito's little brother; my toothless Pomeranian, who looked like a tiny, orange fluffy-haired fox; Trixie, my border collie who was also known as Ms. Skunk; and, last but not least, Mr. Perfect, my Henry Thomas, who looked like a panda bear crossed with a dog. I mean, really, they were all so incredibly lovely. My heart overflowed with pride for my wonderful, beautiful animal family.

He said, "So you rescue animals? I have to tell you what happened to me a few months ago. It was insane." He went on to tell me his story.

"I rent a house with a guy named Dan. When his mom died, he inherited her cat, Smokey. I had never lived with a cat, but this little guy was awesome. He had long, gray fur and green eyes, purred super loud, and was way smart. We watched TV for the ski report every morning while eating breakfast. Sometimes Smokey would hit me in the face with his huge tail, reminding me to save him some milk from my cereal bowl. He was a confident guy, if you know what I mean.

"Dan never seemed to like him. He worried about him from the minute he brought him home. I told Dan, 'Let me take care of him.' So, Smokey slept with me every night. I fed him his brekky and din-din and brushed his long hair so it wouldn't get matted. Smokey and I were tight. My cool little buddy was the best roommate I'd ever had.

"Last month, there was a knock on our back door. It was my neighbor who feeds Smokey when we're out of town. He's kind of a redneck—he always wears camouflage, you know, hunting clothes. He likes my little buddy. The guy asked me where Smokey was, and I said, 'You don't need to feed him, I just fed him.'"

I interjected, "Let's call that guy Mr. Camo for the remainder of the story."

He nodded his head and went on, "Then the guy said, 'I'm not here to feed Smokey; I'm here to take him away. Where is he?' Something was off because the guy was not acting normal. He seemed like he was in a hurry. Then Mr. Camo said, 'Let's just say I've been paid to make him disappear.'

"I got really upset and said, 'Hey, man, you're freaking me out. What are you talking about?'

"Mr. Camo said, 'Dan says that Smokey's deaf and is moving kinda slow, and a quick bullet would be faster than taking him to the vet to be put down.'"

I interrupted—and shot a quick glance at his model-like face and regretted not washing my hair or brushing my teeth. "So, Smokey was his mother's best friend. Maybe Dan had not gotten over her death. Smokey might have been a sad reminder of his mother."

The good-looking hitchhiker nodded, "Oh yeah," and then went on with his story.

I quickly and casually popped a piece of gum in my mouth, put on my huge Jackie O sunglasses, and smiled, indicating for him to continue.

"You know I was flipping out. 'Are you telling me you're going to kill Smokey?' I screamed. 'Hey, dude, if that's what Dan wants, we have to get my little buddy out of here!'

"Mr. Camo sat down, covered his face, and said he couldn't kill Smokey. 'You must think I'm a real idiot. I told Dan that just because I'm a hunter doesn't mean that I kill people's pets.'

"Once I straightened out my redneck neighbor, we came up with a plan to send Smokey to my sister in California, who loves cats and wanted him. I grabbed my Smoker, ran with Camo Man to his house, got online, and bought him a one-way ticket to Cali. The dude actually gave me his $80 hit fee to help buy the ticket and begged me not to tell anyone. Smokey stayed at one of my girlfriend's houses until his flight left for Cali."

Oh great, *one* of his girlfriends? I regretted wasting a piece of gum on the guy. I don't stand in line for a cappuccino, let alone the thought of a boyfriend. The handsome hitchhiker looked pleased with himself as he affectionately stroked Connor's tummy. Connor trustingly rolled over onto his back in the guy's arms and quickly fell into one of his deep sleeps, snoring loudly as the dude laughed and gently bounced him like a baby.

I said, "That's why he's called The Narcoleptic."

The guy held him tighter to his chest and smiled. "I still call my sister to check on Smokey. He really likes his new life on the beach with her and his new cat buddies. She spoils him rotten just like I did." He also said he and his sister had become closer after they completed the cat caper of moving old Smokey to the beaches of California.

I said, "Hiring a hit man for $80 to take out your old cat is a new one for me. Thanks to you, Mr. Camo came to his senses and repented, converting that hit fee for plane ticket money!" I tried to speak his language, ending with a "Way cool, man," but I sounded like an insincere dork. I returned to my normal speech and asked him what he told his roommate about Smokey's sudden disappearance.

He cleared his throat, lowered his voice, and, nodding up and down, said, "You know, I really wanted to tell him what we did. But I decided I'd rather let him sweat it out since he tried to have Smokey whacked. Every day now I tell him how much I miss my little buddy. Someday, after I move out, I'll tell him." He paused and continued to gently bounce Connor on his back, "You want to know something else that's really weird?"

I said, "God, yes! I love animal rescue stories. Keep going." Connor's mouth hung wide open, leaving a tiny wet spot on the sleeve of the dude's ski jacket.

"After that crazy fiasco, Mr. Camo went out and adopted his own gray cat from the shelter. And he named the little guy Smokey! Now, I'm his babysitter when Mr. Camo's out of town. He's a great cat and

I like him, but he'll never take the place of my good friend, the real Smokey Joe."

As if I were Dr. Phil, I interjected, "Well, that may be Camo's passive-aggressive way of getting back at Dan."

He grinned, pulled Connor close to his face, looked into his sleeping eyes, and said, "Yeah man, you know what? Love conquers all."

I smiled and popped another piece of gum into my mouth.

The day I adopted Grace

My Rez Dog, Grace

Photos of dogs flashed on my screen as I searched for a dog to pull from a shelter to foster. It was her pain-filled eyes that instantly caught mine. Her description read as a plea: "It's time she experiences the good things life has to offer." Grace reminded me of my old red border collie, Laney. Her description went on to say she had two toes on her back paw, leaving her with a chronic limp. Half of her tail was missing, and eight of her teeth had broken off at the gums. Starved and unspayed, she bore multiple litters of unwanted puppies. This is the life of a rez dog on the Indian reservations in our country. Her pathetic condition was so heartbreaking that she made what I call "the cut," and I decided to adopt her.

She'd been taken from the Indian reservation in Browning, Montana, by a kind rescue lady who worked with Pintler Pets Shelter in Anaconda, Montana. Pintler Pets had taken a huge load of dogs from Browning, and Grace was on that transport. This big run had put Pintler at full capacity, to the point that they had to double up dogs in the kennels. Some shelters would have said they were too full, but not Pintler. The staff noticed how battered she was and used blankets to make a nice, thick bed in the broom closet for her. She was given free rein in their warm, dilapidated metal building. Finally, she was safe, fed, and protected from the harsh, deep snow and the frigid winter winds in Montana.

They removed her broken teeth, spayed her, and gave her extra meals. She was a favorite of the staff at the shelter. Grace was so appreciative that, according to Pat, the manager, she drooled and howled with excitement when her food dish was filled. Pat also told me that her own house was full of dogs from the rez. "They appreciate everything more than any other dogs. They're my favorites. I'll always take dogs from the rez. They struggle so hard just to survive, and many suffer tragic, painful deaths."

After learning about the shocking animal suffering on the rez, I formed a close relationship with Pat and Phyliss Hargrave, my people at Pintler Pets. Pintler is an underfunded, understaffed shelter of hardworking people in an impoverished area. Pat, and her number-one volunteer Phyliss, have achieved great things with little to no funding.

During this time, I provided in-home care for a lady with dementia. I lived on her 50-acre ranch, and over the course of the ten years I was blessed to live on that magical property, I brought over 200 of Pintler's orphaned animals to my small cabin for foster care. Some were transferred to the AAC, a few animals were provided hospice care, and I personally kept five and made them my family. The majority of them found caring homes in the Jackson area.

My pretty, longhaired, brindled brown girl, Grace, was the first rez dog that came to live with me. She was described as an Australian shepherd mix, but she looked more like a husky or a wolf mix. We all know people and animals with issues. Grace's number-one issue was food. She'd do anything to get it. To stay alive on the rez, she had rifled through trash and killed rodents and, most likely, small game and cats. Most people keep crates in their cars for their dogs to ride in, but not me. I kept a crate in the car to keep my groceries safe when Gracie was a passenger.

Shortly after Grace joined my menagerie, I arrived home one day and found my refrigerator door wide open. The crisper drawers had been dragged into the living room and emptied. A shred of a plastic bag that once held twenty tortillas lay nearby. All that was left of a one-pound block of cheese was the wrapper, strewn like confetti all over the house. There were half-chewed carrots buried under the covers on my bed. Unopened beer bottles were wedged under my kitchen table and chairs. A dozen broken eggs lay neatly in the carton with their shells licked perfectly clean. What little food I'd had for myself was gone.

I'd left a kitchen towel hanging on the refrigerator door handle. She had used that to pull open the door with her mouth. You can bet your last dollar that Conner, my black pug, had been in on the heist and had helped turn it into a real party. He had been known to root carrots from my friend's garden like a little piggy digging for truffles.

A month after I adopted her, Grace hit a new all-time low when she grabbed an unopened metal can of green chilies off the counter. I discovered it in her bed next to her fresh bones and toys, as it dripped juice from her crooked teeth marks. Her dog bed was wet but the chiles were untouched. That's when I reminded myself that those who have nothing many times resort to a life of crime in order to survive. That day she became known as "The Convict."

For her first Christmas, Grace should have been given a case of Slim Fast shakes, a membership to Weight Watchers, and a used treadmill bought from eBay. Don't get me wrong here, I adored my beautiful Grace. Normally I wasn't a poor sport, but I didn't like being outsmarted by a toothless, borderline-chubby dog with a limp.

Like many convicts, Grace was a repeat offender. About four years after she joined my family, she jumped through the window of the house painters' truck, grabbed their small coolers, dragged them into the woods, and gobbled up their lunches as if she was starving. Then, a few days later, about an hour after her breakfast, she got into the window washers' van and inhaled an entire bag of potato chips and a box of Chips Ahoy cookies. Afterward, she innocently sat on the front porch, showing no remorse, and belched like a drunken alcoholic.

As her self-appointed parole officer, I kept rules to follow written in bold red magic marker on yellow Post-it notes on my front door: "CRATE GRACE! NO FOOD ON COUNTER!" My convict reminded me that we can't change people, places, or things—like making an old rez dog that had been starved for years less desperate for food. Ms. Princess Two Toes was a constant reminder that we all have our issues. Grace's behavior issues were nothing compared to how I acted as a troubled teenager. The little amount of grief she caused me didn't come close to what I put my poor mother through. Many times when she did something that annoyed me, I knew it was my pay back for all of the trouble I have caused.

At her first spring shave, my dog groomer buddy Julie was running clippers over Grace's hip when she stopped and said, "Hey Cuppers, I hit something."

I said, "What do you mean you hit something?"

We looked at her shaved hip, which exposed a round piece of metal that had come to the surface of her skin. Julie grabbed a set of pliers, and we pulled out a .22 caliber bullet! We were stunned speechless and looked at each other as I held the bullet in my hand. I finally said, "I've never pulled a bullet out of a dog before."

A few months later, Julie and I had just finished walking our dogs on a bike path when we noticed sheriffs' cars and the Fish and Game officers closing in on us in the parking lot. Puzzled, I said to Jewels, "What in the world is going on here?"

She said, "Maybe there's a cougar or a bear nearby." We quickly put our dogs into our vehicles. I said, "That's got to be it. The bears are waking up now."

I walked up to the officer in a green government uniform. "Hey, how are you? What's going on with all of the officials here?"

In a nervous voice, he asked, "I need to know if you can stay calm."

I said, "Yes, this is about as calm as I get, unless I'm sleeping."

Jewels interjected, "We are pretty calm."

"We had a call that there's an injured wolf in the area."

Jewels and I looked at each other with amusement. I asked, "Who said there's an injured wolf?"

"Well, we got a call at the sheriff's station from a couple of guys who said they had it in the sights on their rifle and were going to take it out for us."

I was floored. "Really? They were going to shoot into a residential neighborhood?"

"We told them if they did, we'd arrest them. Have you ladies seen an injured animal?"

"Well now, wait one minute—I thought wolves were protected," I said.

"No, ma'am, they were delisted from the Endangered Species Act several years ago. Now we have yahoos with guns looking and wanting to shoot them any chance they get."

I said, "Well, can you stay calm now?"

Annoyed, he said, "Oh quit. Now, what have you got?" He was leaning back against my car where Grace lay, deep asleep in her big bed, as she drooled on her blankets.

I said, "I have seen an injured animal."

Jewels casually winked at me and said, "Come to think of it, I did, too."

In a hurried voice, he asked, "Well, where is it? What direction did it go?"

I said, "It's close by. If you turn around and look inside my car, she's sleeping."

"What the heck is going on here, ladies?"

I said, "Well, I have a dog from the rez. She does look a bit like a coyote. Maybe if you're real thirsty for wolf blood, she could look wolfish from a distance. She's had a rough life and walks with a limp. But she *is* a dog. Not a predator unless you're eating a hamburger and not sharing it—then I can't make any guarantees. Her name is Grace. Would you like to meet her? You can see for yourself. I've actually mistaken her for a coyote in my own backyard, especially when the grass is tall and she's out hunting for mice."

He laughed and said, "You're kidding me."

"Normally, yes, but right now I'm not."

He said, "Let me call the guys off and grab my camera."

Grace had been leashed and within ten feet of us on our walk; meanwhile, there was a loaded rifle pointed at her.

The guy laughed when he saw her tongue hanging out of her toothless mouth, "The guys at the department aren't going to believe this one." He apologized and drove off, talking on his phone.

I said, "Thank God they were shut down. If the sheriff hadn't stopped them from taking the shot, they could have killed us or our dogs."

Jewels said, "With the power of a rifle, they could have easily killed innocent people in their homes behind us on the path." She climbed into her truck and said, "You know, Cupper, once again, life is never boring around you."

I said, "Yeah, I guess when we're not pulling a bullet from her hip with a pair of pliers, we're almost dodging them from some redneck who wants to put another one in her."

Grace

Petunia, the Velveteen Pug

Petunia

Okay, one more pug story, and then I'll stop. Over the past two decades, hundreds of dogs, cats, puppies, and kittens have shared my home. They have been all sizes, colors, breeds, dispositions, and peculiar behaviors, and many have had severe medical problems. A few were beloved pets whose owners had died, but most of the animals at shelters had no known history. The only rule in my house has always been no biting. True aggression was never tolerated in my home.

Once I turned fifty, my days of being jumped on and knocked down were over. My tiny house was six hundred square feet, so smaller dogs or disabled animals worked better for me.

Five years earlier, Grace had joined my family. The Pintler Pets Animal Shelter in Montana, where I found her, continued to take animals in dire situations from the Browning reservation, and I constantly checked Pintler's website looking for animals I might foster, transfer to another rescue, train, or help in some way. One day, I clicked on the New Dogs section and saw an older fawn pug. I jumped off my stool and screamed, "Yes!" Then I did my happy dance like Elaine from *Seinfeld* in my kitchen and laughed at myself. My dogs are used to my erratic behavior and rarely lift their heads. I called the manager at Pintler and arranged to foster the old pug.

Her first foster mother, who had pulled her off the reservation, called and filled me in on the pug's story. She had pulled the frightened older dog from a grimy plastic crate stuffed with dirty blankets that had been left in a back yard of an abandoned house. Extremely neglected, the pug weighed a mere eight pounds. She said the old girl had recently had puppies, but they were nowhere to be found.

A friend of mine who was skiing in Montana at the time picked the pug up from the shelter for me. Taking her for her first visit to the veterinarian left me speechless when a $2,000 bill was placed in my right hand and a plastic shopping bag full of medicine in my left. James and his black credit card were long gone.

I thought a little old lady name would suit her best—delicate, old-fashioned, and unique—Petunia, or Tuni for short. My sister liked to call her "Tuna," "Tuna Sandwich," or "Tuna Casserole," and sometimes "Stinky Tuna Boat." My fantastic sister, who I call Sissy Bear, mailed Tuni a glitzy rhinestone black-patent-leather collar to welcome her into our family.

For the first month, Petunia got small meals throughout the day of organic cooked meat, laced with antibiotics, vitamins, and probiotics. Her protruding ribs disappeared and were covered by a stunning, shiny, velvet tan coat.

Petunia took up residency in my bedroom closet in a comfy den created especially for her. Clean, oversized pillows were lined with super-soft blankets, wrapped tightly in a polar fleece electric blanket. All my nest-building skills were acquired under my sister's specific, strict tutelage—she referred to herself as a pillowologist or the cozenator. Tuni was content in her cozy cocoon until someone knocked on my door. Then she shot out like a missile and barked ferociously.

The advice from James, the self-proclaimed pugologist, rang loudly in my head, and so Tuni received repeated compliments on her stunning soft coat several times a day. And, of course, her bling collar. She may have believed that the collar's sparkly glare came from genuine diamonds. If it helped her self-esteem, I'd tell her a little white lie occasionally. After all, she was a pug, not the Pope. Anyone who knows me also knows if the collar had real diamonds, it would have been on eBay in a split second to cover the cost of her vet bill. Expensive gifts given to me were often used to pay vet bills.

Tuni settled into my routine nicely, and once spring finally arrived, so did her desire to go outside. She'd sit with her back against mine as we weeded the garden. Her big, fearful eyes became peaceful and content. She allowed me to carry her and trusted me enough to fall asleep in my arms. She eventually barked with happiness and charged the front door to take our morning walks in the woods.

Her severe mood swings came with a low growl and a five second warning to put her down before she nailed my hand with the few teeth she had left. When she growled, I nervously yelled, "Look out—hot potato!" For Halloween, I thought about wrapping her body in tinfoil with a dab of sour cream on her head and salt and pepper shakers taped to her foiled sides. Overall, she was a bit stingy with kisses, but occasionally she'd give me a quick lick on the back of my hand.

One of my favorite authors, Anne Lamott, wrote a book called *Small Victories*. Tuni had many small victories; becoming healthy and trusting me were just two of them. She often rubbed her lovely harp-seal eyes into my pillow, moaned, and snorted in true pug bliss. Every once in a great while, she'd roll onto her back, twist back and forth, and leave a thick layer of her molting velveteen fur on my bed.

After fostering and then adopting Petunia, I fully understand why people keep a crabby and occasionally snappy dog like my little Ms. Hot Potato.

Right to left: Susie before and after rescue grooming

Making Room for Susie

Whenever I get caught up in the everyday mundane routine of going to work, cleaning the house, and caring for my animals, I inevitably get restless and bored. That's when I know it's time for me to get out of town for the day and see some open country. A short, day-long road trip reminds me that our world is full of beauty with new places to see and explore.

I think most of us in Wyoming feel a strong sense of pride in the place we live. The vast wilderness and wide-open spaces are like no other place on earth. Being in the middle of untouched nature gives me the greatest joy and peace, and calms my soul. In between our small towns are endless miles of sagebrush with antelope, deer, and thousands of loose cattle grazing on the open range. Living out west has given me a feeling of freedom.

Several years after I stepped down as the ED at the AAC, I was headed out on one of my day road trips to Idaho Falls and wondered if I should stop in at the shelter there. With plenty of my own dogs, I didn't really need or want another. The staff were doing a great job running the Center, but sick animals at the Idaho shelter were still being euthanized. I knew I could make room if there was one who really needed me. But it had to be a good fit for me and for my animals, given we were living in such a tiny house.

I had a strong feeling there was a dog in there that needed my help, so I stopped. Her cage card read, "Owner surrender, used as a breeder– Susie." Absolutely mortified at her gruesome condition, I immediately grabbed her out of her kennel and went straight into the supply room where I snatched a clean towel and wrapped her in it. I walked through one more time to make sure there were no more dogs that needed me. Unlike the old days, most of the kennels were empty. Things had drastically changed, with animal-rescue groups regularly taking this shelter's overflow. With dog transfers and many new programs in place, they were saving almost all the dogs.

Not finding anyone else needing a home, I knew this was it—she was mine. On our way out, we stopped at the front desk. Parker had retired a few years back, so the employees were strangers to me. I asked the young girl behind the front desk how long Susie had been there. She said, "Oh, about five days. Oh God, she's a real mess. The other two that came in with her were in even worse shape. We had to put them down right away. We put Susie on our Facebook page, but no one has called for her."

I was dumbfounded and asked, "You took her picture, but you didn't clean her up?" It blew me away that Susie had not been groomed. I wrote down my phone number, taped it behind the front desk, and said, "When you get a dog like her that needs help, please call me. I will pay to get them professionally groomed if no one will volunteer to do it."

When we got into the car, Susie sat on my lap and stared at me. I told her she'd be cleaned up and feeling better in no time. My throat had a big lump and my eyes burned as I fought back the dark thoughts of how she had been treated and what her life must have been like. Her breeding, money-making days were over, and that's when she got ditched like a piece of trash.

I tried to act cheerful when I said, "Now you are my special girl, so for lunch, you're getting a warm grilled chicken sandwich." Susie didn't gobble her food like I did. She chewed slowly, as if she was savoring every bite. She ate like a well-mannered lady.

The next stop was, once again, the Petco grooming department. The bitterly cold wind felt as though it were ripping at my face when I put her inside my coat, and two twenty-dollar bills in my pocket. I hoped it would help push her to the front of the line, since we didn't have an appointment for grooming. Inside, I put the cash in the groomer's hand, uncovered Susie, and begged her to help. Her eyes widened in shock, and she quickly took the dog she was grooming off the table and put Susie in its place.

She said, "Let's get her going. It's going to take a while to get this poor little baby back to feeling like a dog."

I hugged the girl and thanked her. Susie would soon be rid of the disgusting, filthy fur that had clung to her for years. Old memories from my years rescuing in Idaho Falls filled my mind. Had I made hundreds of trips? I would never be able to recollect all the times, and it didn't matter. Rescue was now a household word. Reality TV shows had put the public's eye into the shelters; most people were now fully aware of how crucial it is to adopt. My reflections made me smile, knowing sheltering had changed dramatically since the old days when I had filled my car with countless loads of animals from that shelter.

There was no denying she was quite old and probably a hospice dog. Her time with me would undoubtedly be short, so everything with her had to be extra special. I felt like a proud new mother on a mission once again as I pushed my shopping cart through Petco. Susie needed many things, like quality food, vitamins, a pretty new collar with a tag, and a warm jacket for winter. I also grabbed some soft, yummy, canned food (not that I have ever tried it, but dogs seem to enjoy it) and a few thin sweaters for inside the house, since she would soon be just about naked.

It took nearly two hours for the groomer to get her shaved down to the skin and trim her nails so she could stand on her paws. Under the filthy, burr-ridden fur was a silky white-and-gray purebred shih tzu. When I picked her up, I noticed the large tumors covering her stomach. Luckily, the sweet young groomer had carefully avoided nicking her skin. She helped me put on Susie's new sweater and told me that Susie was tired. I started worrying and knew it was time to head straight back home to see my vet before he closed.

All the way back to Jackson, I kept my car under the speed limit while petting Susie. I repeatedly complimented her on her new sweater and her impeccable manners. I made a promise to her that she would never be alone, dirty, or cold again. "You're my baby now, Susie, and I am your momma. Let me tell you—your momma is going to show you just how fantastic life can be."

We drove straight to my veterinarian's office. Theo was a compassionate doctor and was used to me bringing in older, injured, and neglected animals. Theo ran some tests on Susie, and I quietly admired his caring manner. He said, "She sure is a pretty girl. Let's make her a little more comfortable. Her heart is having some trouble working with the size of these tumors; this medication will make her feel better."

He gently explained that she would probably not survive undergoing a major surgery to remove the tumors, nor being spayed. He also said "I'm sure you can make the remainder of her life happy. She's tired, but she's not suffering. You're the perfect person for her." Then Theo said something that surprised me. "I was wondering if you've noticed the way she looks at you." Theo doesn't normally talk about feelings or show emotion. I often teased him, saying he was like the pragmatic Vulcan Spock from *Star Trek,* who had no emotions. Occasionally, I'd pulled his hat off and searched for pointed Vulcan ears. Theo was right—Susie did stare at me in an unusual way, and her eyes stayed focused on me so long as she was awake. Maybe it was the chicken sandwich that had gotten her attention?

When we finally got back home, Susie was in a deep sleep, and we crawled into bed for a nap. Her eyes were closed, and now I was the one who stared at her in complete disbelief that she was the same dog I had met at the shelter. I shuddered when I thought, What if I hadn't stopped at the shelter?

At this time, I was working with elderly clients in their homes, a profession I began at 14 years old. My elegant older lady named Anne was almost completely paralyzed. She spent long days in a wheelchair or stretched out in her recliner. She had barely spoken any words out loud on my twenty-four-hour shifts. My days were spent with Anne, feeding her, brushing her soft silver hair, bathing her, and usually trying to make her laugh with my inane stories. Anne had two older, retired show cats, with long, fluffy white fur and brilliant blue eyes. Her cats ignored her, and she paid little attention to them when they were in the room with us.

But when Anne met Susie, she suddenly spoke clear words and looked directly at her. She told Susie, "Come up here and sit with me." I had cared for Anne for almost a year and had never heard her speak a full coherent sentence. It boggled my mind when she spoke to Susie and also attempted to pet her new little friend. I would hold Anne's hand and slowly glide it down Susie's back over and over until she smiled. We laughed throughout the day, joined together in our love for our dainty and treasured shih tzu.

After I made room for Susie, she brought extraordinary peace, joy, and a positive focus into Anne's small world. Her presence reminded me that providing hospice care and a final home for her was a gift that blessed both of us.

Closing Thoughts

Words sometimes fail to express how grateful I am for all the wonderful animals and people who have touched my life. My mission to save the lives of homeless animals began over thirty years ago, and although I stepped down from running the Animal Adoption Center, my commitment to that mission hasn't wavered. I continue to foster, volunteer, and gather donations for underfunded shelters. Our country has made enormous strides in the animal welfare movement, but we are not finished until all animals are safe and we have achieved a no-kill nation. My dream to do more for abandoned animals continues with great success at the Animal Adoption Center where over twenty-thousand animals have been spayed, neutered, or adopted.

Thank you for buying this book! A portion of the proceeds will go to underfunded spay and neuter clinics throughout the United States. Before I leave you: the biggest mistake a person can make is to think their contribution may be too small.

I wish you great adventures, happiness, and peace in all your endeavors. Most of all . . . *I hope you enjoyed the show!*

RESOURCES

How You Can Help

Get to know your local shelter and their placement partners: Your local animal shelter accepts every animal that enters the facility regardless of age, health issues, behavior problems, or breed. Placement partners are the rescue groups that assist shelters.

Be a responsible pet owner: Be sure to microchip your animals, keep updated pet identification tags on your pets, spay/neuter, choose to adopt a pet only if you plan to care for them for their entire life. When you commit to your own pets for all of their natural life, you set an example for others.

Donate: Your donations are needed for animals to stay alive. When you donate to an animal welfare group, ask where they need financial assistance. If your concern is with dogs that need training, your gift can help a dog get the training it needs to become adopted. Your financial support can be given specifically to the program in need of your support.

Fostering: Fostering a shelter pet can make the difference between life or death when a shelter is at full capacity. Many animals need a calm, quiet environment to decompress and learn skills to become more adoptable. Becoming a foster parent frees up precious space in rescues and shelters for the incoming dogs, cats, puppies, and kittens.

Walk a shelter dog: There might be opportunities to walk dogs outside. They need fresh air, affection, exercise, and attention. It's also a great way for you to get outside, exercise, and enjoy the fresh air in a new and significant way. Your attention will be greatly appreciated by the dogs that sit in cages or kennels all day.

Love and pet shelter cats: You can set a day each week to volunteer at your local animal shelter to interact with cats and kittens. Remember they are in cages twenty-four hours a day, seven days a week, as they wait and hope for adoption. Your life will be enriched as well as theirs.

Volunteer weekly: What does your local animal shelter or rescue need? Do they need help with cleaning cages or litter pans? Or maybe they need someone to take photos of the animals for social media posts. Find out what they need and commit to helping them by volunteering. Take yourself and a few friends to volunteer each week; it will make a huge difference.

Support high-volume/low-cost spay and neuter programs and clinics: High-volume/low-cost or free spay and neuter programs are the only way we will end the killing, and overpopulation, of unwanted pets. Please make sure your animals are fixed. Find a local nonprofit organization that provides high-volume/low-cost spay-neuter surgeries and make a tax-deductible gift today. The only way we can stop the inflow of unwanted animals is for them not to be born.

Adopt, don't shop: Petfinder.com has photos and full descriptions of animals waiting for adoptions at shelters and rescues. You can also check rescues and shelters to see if they have a Facebook page with available animals listed. If not, you can take pictures on your phone and post them yourself.

Donate to your community cats: Join a local cat initiative to stabilize overpopulation of community cats by promoting a *trap neuter return* program (TNR). These organizations also provide colony management for feral cats and encourage responsible guardianship. They feed and provide medical care, and sometimes housing for community cats. You can help buy food or purchase a cat house, or even make one to ensure your community cats have shelter.

Fund a rescue group: Besides your animal shelter, there are many independent groups dedicated to rescuing dogs, cats, rabbits, birds, horses, and farm animals. Shelters, rescue groups, and sanctuaries are essential in the long-term care of animals. When you make a gift to one of these groups, you are helping homeless pets by providing them with the care they need. Most rescue groups need funding, so give today.

Donate needed items: Before dropping off your unwanted items please ask your shelter what they currently need. It may be dog and cat supplies, blankets, towels, wash cloths, office supplies, or donations for vaccinations, etc. Please remember to thank the hardworking staff who are usually underpaid and overworked.

Help organize an adoption event: Work with your local animal shelter or rescue to create a successful mobile adoption event. Do you have a highly visible location for the shelter animals to be seen? Mobile adoptions take animals out into the community and into the eyes of the public. Many shelters need help placing their cats and dogs, and adoption events provide the exposure they need to be adopted or fostered.

Transport: This is an easy way to help animals. Volunteer to transport newly rescued animals to the vet, a local rescue group, a foster parent, or an adopter. Speak with your local animal rescue organization or shelter and ask if they need assistance with transporting animals.

Help with fundraising events: Is your local animal shelter or rescue hosting a fundraising event? If so, ask how you can get involved and help. Maybe it's donated items they need, or maybe they need you to sell tickets to their event. Ask where your efforts are best put to use.

Gather donations on your birthday: Help save lives by collecting donations for your favorite animal rescue charity, instead of receiving birthday gifts on your special day. It's also a great way to celebrate the birthdays of your pet-loving friends, family members, neighbors, and relatives. Social media platforms such as Facebook and Instagram allow you to make donations to help animals in need.

Donate Kuranda dog beds and cat towers: Donate a Kuranda dog bed or a cat tower to an animal shelter or rescue group. The beds are almost indestructible and provide comfort to the cats and dogs that are waiting to be adopted by keeping them off concrete floors. Kuranda has established a discount program that makes it easy for people to donate their products specifically to shelters. A Kuranda drive can be a fun project at your workplace, for your family, your neighborhood, or your friends. When you go to sleep at night you will know animals are more comfortable thanks to your efforts, love, and concern. https://kuranda.com/donate

AmazonSmile: Use Smile.Amazon.com and sign up to support your favorite animal rescue or shelter. This is an easy and free program that will donate to your charity every time you use AmazonSmile to make a purchase. So, sign up today.

Donate pet carriers and crates: Donate clean, new, or gently used pet crates to animal shelters and rescues. Pet carriers are always needed and appreciated.

No Kill Information

The No Kill Advocacy Center is a legal advocacy organization that reforms shelters through litigation, legislation, education, consultation, training, and other direct assistance. The following information is taken directly from nokilladvocacycenter.org with special thanks to Nathan Winograd.

A LIFESAVING DIFFERENCE

WHY SOME SHELTERS KILL & OTHERS DON'T

THE PROGRAMS OF THE NO KILL EQUATION·	NO KILL SHELTER	TRADITIONAL KILL SHELTER
RESCUE PARTNERSHIPS	✓	
VOLUNTEERS	✓	
FOSTER CARE	✓	
COMMUNITY CAT/DOG STERILIZATION	✓	
PET RETENTION	✓	
COMPREHENSIVE ADOPTION PROGRAM	✓	
PUBLIC RELATIONS/COMMUNITY INVOLVEMENT	✓	
MEDICAL & BEHAVIOR PREVENTION & REHABILITATION	✓	
HIGH-VOLUME, LOW-COST STERILIZATION	✓	
PROACTIVE REDEMPTIONS	✓	
HARD-WORKING, COMPASSIONATE SHELTER DIRECTOR	✓	

· Programs must be implemented comprehensively so that they replace killing.

nokilladvocacycenter.org

Two decades ago, a No Kill community was little more than a dream. Today, it is a reality in many cities and counties nationwide, and the numbers of participating communities continue to grow. And the first step is a decision by a shelter's leadership: a commitment to reject kill-oriented ways of doing business, to replace a regressive, anachronistic 19th century model of failure with 21st century innovations by implementing the No Kill Equation. No Kill starts as an act of will.

Animals enter shelters for a variety of reasons and with a variety of needs, but for over 100 years, the "solution" has been the same: adopt a few and kill the rest. The No Kill Equation provides a humane, life-affirming means of responding to every type of animal entering a shelter, and every type of need those animals might have. Some animals entering shelters are community cats. At traditional shelters, they are killed, but at a No Kill shelter, they are sterilized and released back to their habitats. Some animals entering shelters are motherless puppies and kittens. At traditional shelters, some of these animals are killed as well. At a No Kill shelter, they are sent into a foster home to provide around-the-clock care until they are eating on their own and old enough to be adopted. Some animals have medical or behavior issues. At a traditional shelter, they can be killed. At a No Kill shelter, they are provided with rehabilitative care and then adopted. Whatever the situation, the No Kill Equation provides a lifesaving alternative that replaces killing.

The mandatory programs and services are for the No Kill Equation are:
- **Community Cat/Dog Sterilization:** Community sterilization programs humanely reduce impounds and killing.
- **High-Volume, Low-Cost Sterilization:** No- and low-cost, high-volume sterilization reduces the number of animals entering the shelter system, allowing more resources to be allocated toward saving lives.
- **Rescue Groups:** An adoption or transfer/transport to a rescue group frees up scarce cage and kennel space, reduces expenses for feeding, cleaning, and killing, and improves a community's rate of lifesaving. Because millions of dogs and cats are killed

in shelters annually, rare is the circumstance in which a rescue group should be denied an animal.

- **Foster Care:** Foster care is a low-cost, and often no-cost way of increasing a shelter's capacity, caring for sick and injured or behaviorally challenged animals, and thus saving more lives.

- **Comprehensive Adoption Programs:** Adoptions are vital to an agency's lifesaving mission. The quantity and quality of shelter adoptions is in shelter management's hands, making lifesaving a direct function of shelter policies and practice. If shelters better promoted their animals and had adoption programs responsive to community needs, including public access hours for working people, offsite adoptions, adoption incentives, and effective marketing, they could increase the number of homes available and replace killing with adoptions. Contrary to conventional wisdom, shelters can adopt their way out of killing.

- **Pet Retention:** While some surrenders of animals to shelters are unavoidable, others can be prevented—but only if shelters work with people to help them solve their problems. Saving animals requires shelters to develop innovative strategies for keeping people and their companion animals together. And the more a community sees its shelters as a place to turn for advice and assistance, the easier this job will be.

- **Medical & Behavior Programs:** To meet its commitment to a lifesaving guarantee for all savable animals, shelters need to keep animals happy and healthy and keep animals moving efficiently through the system. To do this, shelters must put in place comprehensive vaccination, handling, cleaning, socialization, and care policies before animals get sick, and rehabilitative efforts for those who come in sick, injured, unweaned, or traumatized.

- **Public Relations/Community Involvement:** Increasing adoptions, maximizing donations, recruiting volunteers, and partnering with community agencies comes down to increasing the shelter's public exposure. And that means consistent marketing and public relations. Public relations and marketing are the foundation of a shelter's activities and success.

- **Volunteers:** Volunteers are a dedicated "army of compassion" and the backbone of a successful No Kill effort. There is never enough staff, never enough dollars to hire more staff, and always more needs than paid human resources. That is where volunteers make the difference between success and failure and, for the animals, life and death.

- **Proactive Redemptions:** One of the most overlooked opportunities for reducing killing in animal control shelters is increasing the number of lost animals returned to their families. This includes matching reports of lost animals with animals in the shelter, rehoming animals in the field, and use of technology such as posting lost animals on the internet.

- **A Compassionate Director:** The final element of the No Kill Equation is the most important of all, without which all other elements are thwarted—a hardworking, compassionate animal control or shelter director not content to continue killing, while regurgitating tired clichés about "public irresponsibility" or hiding behind the myth of "too many animals, not enough homes."

While shelter leadership drives the No Kill initiative, it is the community that extends the safety net of care. Unlike some of the traditional shelters—which may view members of the public as adversaries and refuse to partner with them as rescuers or volunteers—a No Kill shelter embraces the people in its community. They are the key to success: they volunteer, foster, socialize animals, staff offsite adoption venues, and open their hearts, homes, and wallets to the animals in need. The public is at the center of every successful No Kill shelter in the nation. By working with people, implementing lifesaving programs, and treating each life as precious, a shelter can transform itself.

Please visit The No Kill Advocacy Center's website for more detailed information.

Acknowledgments

I extend my love, appreciation, and deepest gratitude to the Co-founders of the Animal Adoption Center—Linda Osborne and Tom Patricelli, along with our special volunteers Amanda Gates and Krystal Hoffman. My incredibly skilled, kind mentor and guiding force of thirty years— Clare Payne Symmons. To Anne Jacobson, Krissy Goetz, Heather Mathews, Kara Pollard with Sydney and Skiffy, Krista La Pier, Martha Anderson, Carrie Boynton, and Stephan Fodor (and Dingo)—thank you. I'm so grateful for the wonderful Doctors of Veterinary Medicine I have had the honor of knowing through the years—Dr. Ken Griggs, along with wonderful Carol Cully; Dr. Ernie Patterson; Dr. Heather Carleton; Dr. Joe Wiseman; Dr. Katherine Luderer; and Dr. Theo Schuff.

I couldn't have done this work without my supportive, encouraging friends—Tali and Bob Crozer; Pat Kidder, my cheerleader; Debbie Fox, who has also helped me foster more than a hundred animals; my buddy Phyliss Hargrave; Barb Zimmer; Kelly Neubauer; Katie Schoofs; Chris Vest, the man who created the concept design for the cover of my book; Kechon and Andy Olpin; Jim and Marge Brindley; Birdie Rossetter; Friends at Trail Creek Boarding in Driggs, Idaho; Pam Boyer; Gabby Graves; Sydney Wilcox.

My gratitude to Elizabeth Lopeman who helped made this book a reality. Thank you for managing me!

I appreciate the support from Laura Pitney at Launch My Book, Inc. for helping me with her perfect edits and incredible patience.

Finally, to Papa, Mama, Sissy Bear, brother Allen, and Cousin Liz, thanks for all the needed prayers.

Referrals

For information on how you can help homeless animals, please visit these organizations.

No Kill Advocacy Center: nokilladvocacycenter.org
6114 La Salle Avenue 837
Oakland, CA 94611
The No Kill Advocacy Center is a legal advocacy organization that reforms shelters through litigation, legislation, education, consultation, training, and other direct assistance. The No Kill education programs and services are proven to save the lives of all abandoned animals.

Best Friends Animal Society: Bestfriends.org
5001 Angel Canyon Road
Kanab, UT 84741-5000
Phone: (435) 644-2001
Email: info@bestfriends.org
Best Friends Animal Society is an animal welfare organization focused exclusively on ending the killing of dogs and cats in America's shelters. Best Friends runs the nation's largest no-kill sanctuary for companion animals, as well as lifesaving programs in collaboration with its nationwide network of members and partners working to save them all. They have pledged to take our country to no-kill by 2025.

Alley Cat Allies: alleycat.org
7920 Norfolk Avenue Suite 600
Bethesda, MD 20814-2525
Phone: (240) 482-1980
When it comes to cat advocacy, Alley Cat Allies is working in communities to champion low-cost spay and neuter policies and programs, as well as the lifesaving *trap neuter return* (TNR) program. Once viewed as radical new concepts, these humane cat protocols are now mainstream. They are a resource for tens of thousands of dedicated cat caregivers, advocates, nonprofit groups, and volunteers driving change and accelerating protection for millions of cats worldwide. You can find TNR stories on my website: iwilltakeyouhome.com

Animal Adoption Center—Spay/Neuter Wyoming Program
270 East Broadway
Jackson, WY 83001
Mailing address: P.O. Box 8532
Jackson Hole, WY, 83002
Phone: (307) 739-1881
animaladoptioncenter.org
E-mail: adopt@animaladoptioncenter.org

Important Disclaimer: Rebecca Tinnes currently acts as an independent animal advocate to animal shelters and rescues to help them increase their lifesaving efforts. (She is not currently associated or affiliated with any specific group.)

Made in the USA
Monee, IL
28 April 2022

95596215R00105